Modern Mutual Fund Families & Variable Life
Tools for Investment Growth and Tax Benefits

Modern Mutual Fund Families & Variable Life

Tools for Investment Growth and Tax Benefits

By
Carl E. Andersen

and
James B. Ross

DOW JONES-IRWIN
Homewood, Illinois 60430

This publication is designed to provide accurate and authoritative information in regard to the subject matter covered. It is sold with the understanding that the publisher is not engaged in rendering legal, accounting, or other professional service. If legal advice or other expert assistance is required, the services of a competent professional person should be sought.

From a Declaration of Principles jointly adopted by a Committee of the American Bar Association and a Committee of Publishers.

Acquisitions editor: Richard A. Luecke
Production manager: Carma W. Fazio
Designer: Sam Concialdi
Compositor: Carlisle Communications, Ltd.
Typeface: 11/13 Century Schoolbook
Printer: Arcata Graphics/Kingsport

ISBN 1-55623-050-8

Library of Congress Catalog Card No. 87–71544

Printed in the United States of America

2 3 4 5 6 7 8 9 0 K 5 4 3 2 1 0 9 8

To Kiku and Ann for putting up with us; "Thumper" O'Keefe—tomorrow's investor; and the "Yankee Financial Network" for being patient as we borrowed time due rightly to these great people.

FOREWORD

I met Carl Andersen on a trout-fishing expedition arranged by my wife Phoebe in the spring of 1971. Almost a half-century earlier the stock market came to my attention as a young editor for the *Atlantic Monthly* in Boston. Those, of course, were the years of building frenzy in the securities markets that culminated with the market crash in 1929, and the bank holiday which followed in 1933.

Fortunately for me in that memorable debacle, my good friend in finance, James N. White, a partner in Scudder, Stevens and Clark, saved my small nest egg by persuading me to sell everything a month before the calamity began.

In the early years of my friendship with Carl—while both he and co-author Jim Ross were still active senior officers with Boston's venerable Keystone Custodian Funds—I envied his abilities on the salmon rivers of Iceland and New Brunswick. In my book, *The Miramichi Salmon Club - A History* (Brunswick Press, 1984), I noted "the master Carl Andersen whose left-handed casts dominated Top of the Falls."

After my long-time advisor and friend Jim White retired from Scudder, Stevens and Clark, I discovered that Carl was a very astute replacement. And, following Boston's famous blizzard in 1978, during which Carl was trapped for five days at the Parker House Hotel, I discovered that he had a flair for writing about investments in general, and mutual funds in particular.

This is the fourth book he has produced since the snows covered New England waist-deep. Each of them makes the often complex issues involved in mutual-fund investing relatively simple for both the financially skilled and those without formal training or experience.

Through almost two decades of friendship with Carl and his lovely wife Kiku, we have shared the delight of salmon camps and trout streams—including some very secret spots!—and regular bridge parties and good dinners filled with conversation.

We also have met many of Carl's Wall Street friends and associates during his annual get-togethers at Sturbridge Village, Boston's Meridien Hotel, and at Newport, Rhode Island.

Jim and Ann Ross came to my attention at the Newport gatherings. Jim, as I soon discovered, is a fellow Harvard alumnus and has compiled a brilliant record in finance and insurance. The only fly in Jim's ointment seems to be his penchant for fishing for brook trout with worms!

In my early glimpses of Wall Street there were a handful of mutual funds. Today, Carl and Jim tell me, there are thousands. Scudder, Stevens and Clark were in the game early, as were the authors' Keystone funds.

Taxes were relatively simple in those early years. Today they are a horror of complexity and confusion. . .more difficult to deal with than selecting the correct color and size of wet or dry fly to raise a great salmon!

My experience had spanned more than six decades, before financial planning was devised to deal with these confusions as well as those created by the unbridled growth in varieties of mutual funds and other securities. Carl tells me that he and Jim Ross probably invented modern "financial planning," but the history book on the subject hasn't been written.

I do know that this book, like Carl's earlier books on mutual funds and financial planning, is written to defuse the investors' and taxpayers' concerns of the moment, simplify the complex, and answer important questions for investors of all types and risk inclination.

The backgrounds possessed by the authors are both immense and rare. Jim with his stints as a senior officer for a bevy of great insurance concerns, and Carl with comparable experience on Wall Street and in the mutual-fund arena, bring more than sixty years of top-grade experience to this book. I expect that readers will enjoy and profit from its reading.

Edward A. Weeks
The Atlantic Monthly Press
Boston, Massachusetts

ACKNOWLEDGMENTS

We desire to record our thanks to "the great ones" of financial innovation and sales. That long, long list includes Agnes, Nick, and Edward Forst; Scane Bowler and Jack Kenney; David Butterfield . . . people who make present and future American families happier and wealthier.

We also recognize that nothing ever happens until the saving and investing public agrees! On that score, thousands would be less wealthy or happy without the knowledge, experience, and unending efforts of our partner Mike Walsh, and our associates David Cichon, Gordon Bowersock, Larry Freed, Bob Fain, Mike Brennan, Milton Spitzbard, and Laurie McCormick.

There are also the great creators and doers in the world of mutual funds. It's not a long list, but certainly it would always include Joel Bernstein, Tom Fellows, Tom Franckhauser, Doug Graney, Harry Kline, Bob Stillman, and others from the old "Keystone Gang" who engineered and delivered much of the boom and change being experienced in financial services today.

And, lastly, those folks like Cathy Buduo and Rhonda Benoit who daily make the wheels roll smoothly for clients and associates, and Michele Andersen and Nancy Gallagher who worked so tirelessly in this effort.

Carl E. Andersen
James B. Ross

CONTENTS

Products and Services: What's Going to Be New?
Variable Life Insurance Offerings. Leverage,
Leverage, Leverage. Services, Services, Services.
Costs, Costs, Costs. Regulation and Taxes.
Conclusions.

PART 1

HISTORY, EVOLUTION, AND MEASUREMENT

CHAPTER 1

CONCEPTIONS AND MISCONCEPTIONS: MUTUAL FUNDS OR VARIABLE INSURANCE CONTRACTS . . . BEGINNING OR END?

"Concentrate on making money in the market, not on making the tape agree with you."

Jesse Livermore

The nearly trillion dollar mutual fund industry has been the subject of numerous books and scholarly studies in recent years. There was a time—the 1970s, for example—when mutual funds were in such distinct disfavor that rarely were they mentioned in the financial and popular press. After all, the promise of easy profit in the "go-go" years of the late 1960s had turned mutual fund assets to much smaller sums in the stock market crash of 1973–74. "Best performance" in those times meant not how much the holder made, but how little was lost!

Presently, readers of magazines catering to such varied publics as airline passengers, dirt bikers, and saltwater fishermen, are treated to annual, monthly, quarterly, and unscheduled statistical reviews of relative results in the mutual fund area. Much of this reporting on and about the venerable and well-established mutual fund industry is, as we will discuss in coming chapters, without merit.

Mutual funds in America are entering their seventh decade. While limping along through the 1970s as a minor player in the muscular realms of banking, insurance, and Wall Street, funds have now conquered center stage and hold it. While mutuals were scorned by bankers and insurers in decades past, and promoted gingerly by Wall Street brokerages as casual but high-profit specialty investments, today these financial titans struggle to control the mutual fund industry, and to bring their considerable fiscal and financial muscle to the marketing sector. It seems mutual funds (and with them considerable control of investor assets) comprise the best game in town.

In historic terms, the mutual fund industry in America commenced in the early 1920s with names like Massachusetts Investment Trust (today, Massachusetts Financial Services, a unit of Canada's Sun Life), Pioneer Fund, and the Investment Trust of Boston.

These originals—by-products of counterparts in Great Britain and elsewhere a century earlier—were funds based on common stock with a particular eye to the pillars of industry: blue chips and the occasional near-stellar stock. The first funds devoted to managing bonds did not appear until a decade later when the Keystone Custodian Funds were formed.

In those halcyon pre-1929 times, these new open-end mutuals were a negative invention when compared to the great trusts and closed-end funds created in the years prior to the Great Crash. These closed-end funds bought industries such as electric utilities and, believe it or not, match-making. In the case of the open-end mutuals, all survived in some form; in the case of the closed-end funds, many failed to survive in either name, or asset terms when the investors are considered.

Both types offered the investor a similar and striking set of ideas:

- Pooling of small investors' assets to accomplish the money-making goal by hiring skillful management.
- Broad diversification of assets, to assure significant winnings when selection was correct, and the spreading out of losses when a bad or nonperforming investment found its way into the portfolio.

Thus, with small amounts of capital, the saver and investor could participate in the seemingly endless growth of American capitalism. These collective small sums could buy the wisdom and shrewdness of great business minds. And—relish the thought—all would be well when the tidy profits were divided among the multitudes!

LEVERAGE AND IOUs

The basic difference between these early mutual funds is concentrated in the leverage and IOU equation. The open-end funds, still leaders in the fund industry today, tended to avoid borrowing (leverage in the IOU sense) and broadly diversified themselves over many industries.

The closed funds, conversely, used ample access to the IOU. In addition, these investment vehicles almost always focused on specific industry areas. Electric utilities were mentioned earlier, but real estate also comes to mind. Many of these performed a vanishing act in the horrible 1930s. The problems were too much debt with interest payments due to survive crisis times, and usually too much emphasis on a troubled industry sector.

The broadly diversified funds, without leverage or industry focus, not only survived but paid dividends in some form throughout the most devastating economic time in memory. We report these points not with specific and personal memory of the events, but through the eyes of Ted Weeks, author of this book's Foreword, who served as editor of the *Atlantic Monthly* throughout that era's boom-bust-recovery period.

IN THE 1930s . . . AND BEYOND

That a mutual fund's management could and would manage a portfolio of bonds is hardly a new idea. Keystone Custodian Funds, once a Philadelphia operation that moved to Boston for reasons unknown, began to offer bond and other "fixed income" mutual funds in 1932. Thus the hottest Wall Street selling themes in the 1980s were born 50 years earlier.

FIGURE 1–1
Industry Sectors Offered By Fidelity Funds

Air Transport	Electronics	Precious Metals
American Gold	Energy	Property & Casualty
Automation/Machine	Energy Services	Regional Banks
Automotive	Financial Services	Restaurant Industry
Biotechnology	Food & Agriculture	Retailing
Broadcast & Media	Health	Savings & Loan
Brokerage	Health Care Delivery	Software
Capital Goods	Housing	Technology
Chemicals	Industrial Materials	Telecommunications
Computers	Leisure	Transportation
Defense	Life Insurance	Utilities
Electric Utilities	Paper & Forest	

The innovative rage in this modern fund era, judging at least from the advertising budgets of asset managers who are "reinventing the stock market," is the *sector fund*. A sector fund, in terms of management philosophy, resembles the non-diversified industry funds that met with abrupt demise in the financial holocaust of the 1930s.

Thus Fidelity Funds, the present leader in the sector area, currently offers the stock market in 35 industry slices or sectors, as displayed in Figure 1–1. And Fidelity advertises far and wide that these funds represent a new way to play the stock market!

Sector funds are, however, hardly new. A concern known as Group Securities managed mutual funds in the late 1930s through the early 1960s with specific industry focus on—perish the thought—tobacco, steel, oil, aircraft, and so on. There really is little new where asset management and mutual funds are the subject matter, except in semantics, distribution, federal regulation, costs of ownership, and taxation.

SEMANTICS

When is a mutual fund a mutual fund, and when is a mutual fund really a life insurance policy or an annuity contract? These are key questions (targeted for later chapters) as the cost of ownership—the price you will pay—can vary significantly when a mutual fund, or family of funds, is reshaped to fit within the insurance contract.

Costs or prices can be altered in the conceptual reconfiguration of a mutual fund family within an insurance policy. The taxation on income streams generated by the underlying funds also can be reconfigured. Thus, in the complicated world of investment and taxation, one approach will be better for one family situation, and another better for other situations. Splitting computer chips and fiscal hairs is a tedious game, but every individual circumstance will require review to find the right choice.

The marketing of mutual funds, and the variable insurance contracts that encapsulate mutual funds, has also been altered dramatically in the previous decade.

Wall Street wirehouses viewed mutual funds as "has beens" for years. They simply tolerated funds—a minor part of their offerings to investors—as a means of generating higher commissions for retail brokers, and forcing the fund managements to trade, through them, significant volumes of the stocks and bonds in their growing portfolios. There were many precursors of Ivan Boesky in the decades that preceded brokerage discounting. These carpetbaggers were the Wall Street folks who could get the retail salespeople to sell mutual funds and then use that sales leverage to persuade managements to trade stocks with them!

In the modern era we find virtually all major stock brokers creating funds of their own. The brokerage firms find that "assets under management," with daily management fees generated, is a far better idea than trading stocks in a world of discount-brokerage commissions. "The game now," as one brokerage-firm mogul related, "is control of client assets. We are even prepared to lose considerable sums to get that control!"

Obviously, the life insurance industry, in its stodgier fashion, has come to a similar conclusion. The salespeople simply cannot continue to sell "ordinary" or "whole" life insurance where the insurance company and salesperson appear to make a disproportionate share of the money. The marketplace—the saving and investing public—deserves something perceived as a better shake. Thus by far the fastest growing financial phenomena of the 1980s through the next decade—or until Uncle Sam sharpens his pencil—are the variable life insurance/annuity contracts. These contracts are based on a mutual fund family set up within an insurance policy . . . or, viewed from the other side, they are well-thought-out insurance contracts closely integrated with policyholder assets but separated from the general account of the insurance company.

A WORKING DEFINITION

Throughout the book, the example of a variable life product will be the single-premium variable life insurance policy. Insurance companies offering this product define it early in their documents, most often by comparing and contrasting this variable form of the product with a traditional "fixed-benefit," single-premium whole life insurance policy. These are typical comparisons and contrasts taken from the Crown America offering:

> The single-premium variable life insurance being offered by Crown America is, in many respects, similar to traditional "fixed-benefit" single-premium whole life insurance. In other respects, it is quite different.

> **The Main Similarities Are:**

> - The Policyowner pays a single premium for a Policy that provides a death benefit which is payable to the beneficiary upon the insured's death.
> - A minimum death benefit is guaranteed.
> - The Policy has a cash value that the Policyowner may obtain by surrendering the Policy.

> **The Main Differences are:**

> - The Policyowner may allocate the Policy's investment base to one or more of the seven investment Sub-Accounts of the Crown America Variable Life Separate Account, to the fixed-rate option (funded by Crown America's General Account), or both. The Sub-Accounts are the Money Market, Bond Income, Capital Growth, Managed, and three Zero Coupon Bond Sub-Accounts with maturity years of 1991, 1996, and 2006. Each Sub-Account

invests in the shares of a distinct mutual fund portfolio of the Crown America Series Fund, Inc.

* The death benefit under a Policy can increase or decrease annually depending on the investment performance of the investment Sub-Accounts to which the Policy's investment base is allocated; but the death benefit will never decrease below the guaranteed minimum face amount of the Policy if there is no outstanding Policy loan.
* The Policy offers the opportunity for appreciation of its net cash value based upon investment results. The cash value may increase or decrease as of each valuation day. When the premium is allocated to the Sub-Accounts, it is possible, if investment results are unfavorable, for the cash value to decrease to zero; the Policyowner bears the total risk of decreases in the cash value, since no minimum amount is guaranteed.

We will refer to these differences throughout the text, since all are rooted in the variable nature of the contract. Clearly, the policyowner may control the allocation of the moneys he has invested in the investment base of the contract; the death benefit varies with underlying fund performance; and the cash value varies with underlying fund investment performance as well. All are features that the investor seeks in his or her life insurance contract.

AND . . . TAXES

The present tax act (if it lives as long in its present shape as previous acts, it will be history before you read this page) advantaged life insurers in very meaningful ways. The conventional mutual fund holder—unless he or she has invested in an Individual Retirement Plan, pension, or other retirement vehicle qualified under law—can be disadvantaged at least five ways when contrasted with the same owner of the variable insurance contract, who may have within his insurance contract perfect clones of the original funds.

A later chapter will deal with the specifics of these tax breaks which, while they last, may be the best savings and investment vehicles of this or coming decades—if you believe, as we do, in the pyramiding and compounding power of mutual funds.

REGULATION

Every basic text on mutual funds—those that your sons and daughters read in college (or set aside while watching the "soaps")—mentions in glowing detail why Congress passed the Investment Companies Act of 1940. Keep in mind the earlier differences between leveraged and unleveraged funds—some borrowed money, often to excess, and others did not borrow at all. Also, to be consistent, some mutual funds were targeted on a specific industry, and therefore lacked true economic diversification.

The " '40 Act," following the devastating era of the 1930s, legislated the best elements and particulars of mutual funds to benefit the largest possible audience. Without belaboring the details, the act said:

- Mutual funds will be diversified.
- The funds prospectus will detail a specific investment goal: growth, income, safety of capital, etc.
- To qualify, mutual funds will give full disclosure of costs, investment policy, third-party custodianship of moneys, and invested assets;
- The people who run the funds—trustees or directors—will include "nonaffiliated" parties; i.e., folks who are interested in your well-being, not the self-interest of managements present and future.

These requirements are heady, indeed! They are quite unlike the regulations that apply to banks and life insurers. The funds must provide full disclosure in every regard. They must even report promptly on failures and disasters. Every reader is aware of spectacular examples in the public press of contrary behavior by significant banks and insurers.

More importantly, mutual funds must do as described: assemble a board of outsiders to monitor activities, assure broad diversification, publish audited results, hire managers to invest shareholder funds, and keep assets—cash and investments—in the hands of a trusted third party, usually a bank or trust company. When you consider charge cards, brokerage accounts, car loans, and other credit transactions of size, the " '40 Act" appears to be a major stepping stone in protecting your personal and financial interests.

Of course, in performing those functions for shareholders, a lot of complex bookkeeping and tax–record-keeping is an often-overlooked byproduct. That tax-record and scorekeeping for fund investors may be one of the true bargains available from Wall Street these days.

AND NOW, THE BANKS

So, what began as a grouping of entrepreneurs in asset management attempting to access the general public's "small sums," has become an industry in the United States of America that dwarfs the much-discussed "third-world debt." It's a trillion dollars or so, at the moment, and rising fast . . . but for your benefit or theirs?

With insurance companies and stock brokerages entering the scene in droves, it will not be long before the banking community enters the fray. Since the 1930s bankers have been excluded specifically from the world of Wall Street underwriting and mutual funds. Yes, they did have their trust departments to manage stock and bond investments for corporate or wealthy individual clients. And again, they could be involved in certain municipal-bond and government-financing transactions. However, they were shut out from the mutual fund arena because they could not, under federal law, underwrite the shares; and from the variable-insurance area because they were banks, not insurance companies!

There has been a progressive mellowing in federal and state banking. The "bank holding company" took shape a decade ago. Savings banks and savings and loan associations have increasingly taken shape as public corporations. Federal law, enacted in the 1930s, has waffled. With this strengthened position vis-à-vis federal law, and effective and powerful banking competition from our foreign friends, banks will become major players in mutual fund management and related fields.

Historically, banks, like life insurers, have been mediocre competitors in the asset-management business . . . at least where the investor seeks better-than-average results, be they from stocks or bonds. One can only conjecture why results have been poor, but a first surmise could be that these venerable and venerated institutions were excluded from the "full disclosure" provisions contained in that wonderful " '40 Act."

Where banks and savings institutions have become very active in recent years is in the sale of mutual funds to depositors. Hundreds of banks have set up financial-planning departments.

These, using licensed brokers, have become a major factor in bringing the mutual fund story to millions of Americans who were unaware of the benefits in fund ownership. This has evolved in less than a decade. Prior to that banks and thrifts were arch-enemies where mutual funds were concerned.

ANGLING FOR THE BEST DEAL

"The only thing for a man to do when he is wrong,
is to be right by ceasing to be wrong."

Jesse Livermore

Over the decades, mutual funds were purchased either through a broker dealer or by mail. Broker dealers varied from huge national brokerages of the Dean Witter or Merrill Lynch stripe, to local companies whose names sounded more like law or accounting firms.

In more recent times the process of purchasing funds, like the process of trading in the securities markets themselves, has been shrouded in obfuscation and growing confusion.

The two original major sources for purchasing mutual funds remain the same. For most of us the dichotomy seems clear: Purchases by mail are "no-load," while purchases through the friendly broker involve a sales expense, or "load." However, the sources of supply are changing, as is the concept of "load" or "sales charge."

Traditionally, the major "eastern mutual" life insurers scorned mutual funds. ("Eastern mutuals" are the giant, old-line sellers of life insurance and annuities often based in Hartford, New York, Boston, and Philadelphia. Metropolitan, John Hancock, and Prudential are representative.) Today, these large carriers have become a driving force where mutual funds are concerned, as we will see when we explore the myriad offerings of variable insurance and annuity products.

Banks and trust companies, once aloof and quite critical whenever and wherever "those mutuals" were discussed, are now active players in the sales game. Trust operations, such as Republic Bank in New York, employ mutual funds instead of stocks and bonds to fund personal trusts and retirement-plan accounts. Discount-brokerage affiliates of savings banks, savings and loans, and, likely soon, credit unions offer mutual funds as part of the discount-brokerage facility.

Associations such as the American Association of Retired Persons, or the Lutheran Brotherhood, not only promote mutual funds to members, but manage mutual funds specifically designed for their constituencies. This appears to be a growing trend with banks, thrifts, insurers, and retailers.

It is possible, tracing the trends in the mutual fund industry, and the proclivity to "follow the leader," that a real estate developer will some day invent the quintessential niche product: "cul-de-sac" funds for buyers living in turn-arounds!

Mutual funds are principally purchased through two mechanisms:

1. Brokerage firms, financial planners, and related parties account for 65 percent of mutual fund sales, excluding money market or cash-like funds.
2. Mutual funds that offer, or presume to offer, no-load (no sales charge) opportunities account for the remaining 35 percent of sales.

Within that balance—65/35 . . . load/no load—are enough variations to confound a Bach at the keyboard, or an Izaak Walton casting to a new body of water.

Our friend Ted Weeks, alive when mutual funds were born, reminds us that one will "cast 1,000 times" before the sea-run Atlantic salmon "takes the fly!" But there are almost 2000 mutual fund variations and configurations, and Ted did not remind us that deciding questions such as who? when? how? where? discount or not? load or not? involves as many options as there are fly patterns in his box . . . or shallow pools as may hold salmon in his rivers. However, Ted, even in his 80s, purchased shares in a growth mutual fund with upscale investment objectives.

Suffice it that mutual funds are available for the larger audience throung virtually every distribution mechanism in our economic system. We even conceive of the day when Blue Cross or the new HMOs will give you a mutual-fund share of your choice when you sign on . . . or the homeowners' insurer will credit your mutual-fund balance when you have no claims for a given year!

And, as we explore commission costs and annual expenses of ownership, we discover quickly that the old idea that funds bought by mail are "no-load" has vanished, and that today no-load funds are often offered by brokers and financial planners.

Mutual funds were once dull stuff, like fishin' with worms for catfish. The innovations in design and distribution in the past decade have been so incredible that the smartest and most knowledgeable investors now stream eagerly to the relative simplicity of mutual funds.

CAST WHERE THE FISH ARE!

"Load" versus "no-load" is a philosophic rather than economic question. If you were about to cast a lure on a large body of water—for example, the Columbia or Gaspé—and you had prepared yourself months in advance for this presumed relaxation, would you wish to cast the lure to water that holds fish, or to water devoid of *Salmo salar* and other great catches?

Mentor Weeks reminds us, as an original mutual fund shareholder, and a mutual fund shareholder for more than 65 years, that "casting the fly is everything . . . but casting to the known fish is much more than that!" And, great man that he is, he might also remind us that it is the profit that counts, not the price printed on the admission ticket . . . or, the enjoyment of profit, great music, art, or literature; not the cost of sheetmusic, pictures, or books.

HOW MANY FISH ARE THERE?

Figure 1–2 illustrates only the funds that the Lipper organization tallies and keeps score on. At this writing, 1,179 funds are measured. Possibly an equally large number of funds are so new or so small that they are not included as yet in the Lipper universe. So, as mentor Weeks might remark, "There certainly are a lot of fish to cast for. Which one is best?" We will deal with those questions as we move into Chapters 2 and 3, and work toward the investment strategy sections later on.

The Lipper tally in Figure 1–2 does not reflect the growth in and proliferation of new closed-end mutual funds and unit trusts. Some recent closed-end funds (funds that are traded in the securities markets rather than offered and repurchased by the fund sponsor at net asset value) have been marketed in the billion-dollar range.

AND WHAT WILL IT COST?

In mutual fund investing, considering and selecting from the thousands of choices is one key element. But the frantic development of new funds obscures the equally frenetic evolution of new methods of charging investors. The once simple load-versus-no-load mix is now obscured by a gaggle of complex loadings, and ongoing management-fee choices.

- There are 12b-1 fee programs that increase investor expenses to allow payment of an ongoing service fee to the dealer or broker that sold you the shares. (Section 12b-1 of the Investment Companies Act of 1940 allows mutual funds to levy a special annual fee against the shareholder

FIGURE 1–2

Lipper Mutual Fund Investment Performance Chart, 3/19/87

LIPPER MUTUAL FUND INVESTMENT PERFORMANCE AVERAGES

Total Reinvested Cumulative Performance

No. of Current Funds	Type of Fund	7/26/84- 3/19/87	6/23/83- 3/19/87	3/20/86- 3/19/87	12/31/86- 3/19/87	3/12/87- 3/19/87
133	Capital Appreciation	+ 97.47%	+ 46.83%	+ 23.38%	+ 24.02%	+ 0.59%
226	Growth Funds	+ 96.88%	+ 60.08%	+ 21.18%	+ 21.85%	+ 0.67%
45	Small Co Grwth	+ 83.96%	+ 38.88%	+ 15.39%	+ 24.55%	+ 0.48%
147	Growth and Income	+ 96.21%	+ 81.95%	+ 20.91%	+ 16.86%	+ 0.59%
39	Equity Income	+ 79.50%	+ 80.64%	+ 16.09%	+ 10.99%	+ 0.56%
590	Gen. Eq Fd Avg.	+ 94.59%	+ 63.65%	+ 20.78%	+ 20.57%	+ 0.51%
7	Health Funds	+ 155.28%	+ 68.74%	+ 35.03%	+ 28.86%	− 0.06%
11	Natural Resources	+ 68.10%	+ 41.19%	+ 34.93%	+ 24.89%	+ 3.32%
26	Sci & Tech.	+ 83.29%	+ 39.60%	+ 26.49%	+ 28.70%	+ 0.35%
8	Utility Funds	+ 105.96%	+ 111.60%	+ 15.80%	+ 4.28%	− 0.20%
39	Specialty Funds	+ 108.35%	+ 87.02%	+ 16.68%	+ 21.35%	+ 0.25%
33	Global Funds	+ 124.40%	+ 101.00%	+ 28.75%	+ 13.98%	+ 0.78%
40	Interntnl Fd	+ 158.99%	+ 150.82%	+ 42.59%	+ 12.38%	+ 1.15%
24	Gld Oriented Fd	+ 47.01%	+ 2.90%	+ 52.74%	+ 30.05%	+ 2.57%
4	Optn Grwth Fd	+ 65.78%	+ 65.61%	+ 15.41%	+ 15.51%	+ 1.56%
19	Optn Inco Fd	+ 55.80%	+ 51.63%	+ 14.76%	+ 11.56%	+ 0.56%
801	All Eq Fd Avg.	+ 95.35%	+ 65.39%	+ 23.19%	+ 20.26%	+ 0.71%
30	Balanced Funds	+ 94.68%	+ 86.27%	+ 19.19%	+ 12.78%	+ 0.44%
19	Income Funds	+ 64.50%	+ 64.69%	+ 13.15%	+ 6.51%	+ 0.35%
329	Fixed Inco Fd	+ 55.82%	+ 61.55%	+ 11.24%	+ 3.48%	+ 0.24%
1179	All Funds Average	+ 85.92%	+ 65.38%	+ 19.70%	+ 15.11%	+ 0.57%
1179	All Funds-Median	+ 85.54%	+ 65.43%	+ 17.98%	+ 15.61%	+ 0.37%
	No fd in Un	706	580	988	1151	1176

Unmanaged Indexes Without Dividends Cumulative Performance

Value 3/19/87						
2299.57	Dow Jones Indus.	+ 107.63%	+ 85.18%	+ 27.45%	+ 21.29%	+ 1.42%
294.08	S&P 500	+ 95.95%	+ 72.41%	+ 24.33%	+ 21.44%	+ 0.98%
337.03	S&P 400	+ 97.93%	+ 74.76%	+ 28.83%	+ 24.85%	+ 1.24%
167.28	NYSE Composite	+ 93.75%	+ 69.26%	+ 22.83%	+ 20.71%	+ 0.80%
337.47	ASE Index	+ 79.60%	+ 38.28%	+ 26.24%	+ 28.18%	+ 1.65%

Estimated Reinvested Unmanaged Indexes Cumulative Performance

Value 12/31/86		12/31/71- 12/31/86	12/31/76- 12/31/86	12/31/81- 12/31/86	12/31/85- 12/31/86	9/30/86- 12/31/86
*331.10	Cnsmr Price Ind	+ 168.97%	+ 89.96%	+ 17.62%	+ 1.13%	+ 0.27%
*1895.95	D J Reinvested	+ 350.12%	+ 222.43%	+ 176.28%	+ 27.25%	+ 8.23%
*242.17	S&P 500 Reinvstd	+ 364.80%	+ 266.46%	+ 147.67%	+ 18.67%	+ 5.57%

Specialized Reinvested Indexes Cumulative Performance

Current Index Value		7/26/84- 3/19/87	6/23/83- 3/19/87	3/20/86- 3/19/87	12/31/86- 3/19/87	3/12/87- 3/19/87
389.11	Lipper Gr Fd Ind	+ 104.33%	+ 67.76%	+ 22.48%	+ 20.43%	+ 0.66%
598.94	Lippr G&I Fd Ind	+ 99.95%	+ 79.68%	+ 23.72%	+ 19.30%	+ 0.60%
492.61	Lipper Bal Fd Ind	+ 96.46%	+ 82.01%	+ 20.79%	+ 14.57%	+ 0.34%
159.44	Lipper Gld Fd Ind	N/A	N/A	+ 44.91%	+ 29.58%	+ 4.02%
165.50	Lipper Sc&Tch Ind	N/A	N/A	+ 23.56%	+ 30.02%	+ 0.07%
244.27	Lipper Intnl Ind	N/A	N/A	+ 38.12%	+ 10.34%	+ 0.85%

The method of calculating total return data on indices utilizes actual dividends on x-dates accumulated for the quarter and reinvested at quarter end. This calculation is at variance with SEC release 327 of Aug. 8, 1972, which utilizes latest 12-month dividends. The latter method is the one used by Standard & Poor's.

Source: Lipper Analytical Sources, Inc.

assets for purposes of advertising and providing services to fund holders. 12b-1 pricing is a very controversial issue at this time.)

- Historically, the load fund was viewed as charging 8 percent in fees to get on board. Numerous funds today are reducing the fee to 4 percent or so. Some are reducing the fee to as little as 2 percent, but combining that lower charge with 12b-1 charges to compensate the broker.
- Some funds advertising as "no-load" levy commissions if the investor sells the shares before a certain time period, often four to six years, elapses.
- A few funds today still charge a sales commission for reinvestment of dividends in additional shares.
- Some funds, typically advertised as no-loads, charge a flat percentage when the shares are sold regardless of the years shares are held.
- Possibly most confusing are the funds that have no sales load when they are not performing well, or getting good press, but slap on a load when the reverse occurs.

Advertising is a theme in some of these points. In reviewing the Sunday *New York Times* financial section, we counted six or more pages of mutual-fund advertising in recent issues with two or more per issue of the full-page variety. *Money,* and other key financial slicks, often have 30 or more pages of mutual-fund advertising. If we were to walk back ten or twenty years and count fund advertising in those times, rarely would the reader find a full page. More than likely, all advertising by funds would not add up to one page for the *Times,* and a few pages for a *Money, Forbes,* or *Barron's,* and then only for the quarterly mutual fund specials!

Much of this advertising explosion, and huge telemarketing and direct-response campaigns unknown in the industry only a decade earlier, is likely funded with those controversial 12b-1 charges. Thus existing shareholders appear to be paying extra for purposes of bringing new holders and assets to the funds! That's good news for Madison Avenue, and great news for the funds and Wall Street brokers that trade fund holdings. It may be both bad and expensive news for shareholders, as funds burgeon in size and become more difficult to manage if they are stock or growth funds.

Usually, loads and ongoing management charges—known in the industry as the "expense ratio"—are published in different parts of the offering prospectus. Thus the investor reading the sales materials and legal prospectus may have some difficulty in putting all of the pieces together.

One ancient but unknown philosopher noted that "nobody ever told you it would be easy!" With the gaggle of charges and changes, and the complex wording in a fund prospectus, the modern mutual fund family is indeed proving that point. Or, as Ted Weeks might say, "Angling for the best deal is sure hard these days."

The questions raised by the ballooning bevy of new mutual funds and new types of funds is, to us at least, dwarfed by the cost question. Is a no-load cheaper to own than a load fund? It may not be when pricing differences are added to the equation, or the fund shareholder plans to stay on board for the long haul.

The typical shareholder in prior decades has typically invested for less than five years. Thus, the 8 percent initial load would add up to 1.6 percent for each year. Added to the normal "expense ratio" of the 1940–80 era of .65–.76 percent, the actual annual cost of ownership for the five year holding cycle was 2.2 percent or more.

The no-load funds of that period—names like T. Rowe Price, Scudder, Loomis Sayles, and others—usually had "expense ratios" of the same size as the loaded funds. Thus the loaded-fund investor owning for five years needed to earn from either dividends or capital gains quite a lot more each year just to catch up with the no-load buyer.

As we will see in Chapter 4—"Portfolio Management & The Capital Market Line"—earning even one additional percent is very difficult work. Many market watchers, huge financial institutions, and business schools that train future analysts and economists believe the task to be impossible!

To further complicate the cost questions, the new variable insurance and annuity products have come on stream. These, in addition to the management fees discussed earlier, have a variety of insurance charges for mortality and other factors. Thus where straight mutual fund costs of ownership are restricted to the commission or load costs and the expense ratio, these variables have a third set of expenses. These will be reviewed in Chapter 8, and the tax impacts as they differ from funds will be reviewed in Chapter 7.

Overall, the charges levied on the shareholder of mutual funds have risen sharply since 1980. A management fee of 1 percent was rare in earlier years; now that percentage, and often much more, is quite common.

A REDEEMING FACTOR

The flip side—Good news for the shareholder!—relates to changes in the costs of buying and selling the stocks held in a fund portfolio.

Prior to 1972 all investors paid the same commission for each 100 shares traded on the major stock exchanges. After that year commissions charged to buy and sell became negotiable. The discount broker, now commonplace, was born in the aftermath. Since mutual funds are often huge buyers and sellers, and Wall Street brokers covet these giant trades, a mutual fund today often pays a fraction of the old charges, or pennies per share when compared with the average brokerage-firm customer.

While impossible to quantify for the fund industry at large, it is safe to assume that actively traded stock and growth mutuals today offset a large portion of the management-fee costs. These huge savings directly reduce the overall expense of running the fund and shave the holders' costs indirectly. In some rare cases these savings may offset all of the management fees.

It should be noted that stock, growth, and other types of funds owning large portfolios of stocks—sector funds, for example—were singled out for the commission-savings analogy. Bond and income funds are often less active traders than stock funds. Also, bond funds may often purchase newly issued bonds— "syndicate items," as they are called on Wall Street. These are not usually discounted.

Thus when considering purchase of a mutual fund or variable insurance contract, or in selecting a modern mutual fund family as a long-term vehicle for savings, income, blue-chip investment, and growth, there are many variables. These, to summarize, include:

- What is the sale charge or loading structure?
- Is the load on the front-end, or back-end, or is the fund a true no-load?
- Is the management fee average, low, or high?
- Does the overall "expense ratio" include 12b-1 payments for the fund and the soliciting broker?
- If the instrument is a variable life or annuity contract, are the mortality costs in line with industry averages?

Of course, the record of management's stewardship of the invested assets is a critical step in the selection process. If the managers are doing a wonderful job they are entitled to better compensation than the mediocre manager. Thus before making a final decision based on costs alone, the fund family should be looked at closely in terms of investment results. Chapter 3 will deal with this issue in more detail.

SHOULD YOU BE INVESTING IN MUTUAL FUNDS?

Do you have the stomach for risk? A short test may help you answer that key question. After all, what happens to your money on a daily basis can have a large psychological effect!

1. Would you find yourself "scared" by every newscast or headline that said the market was down?
2. Would scare headlines make you want to sell your mutual funds?
3. Do you have a "Type A" investment personality? (Cardiac prone!)
4. Do you have a huge ego? Are you able to admit freely to losing in a declining stock market?
5. Does it bother you to lose money no matter how small the amount?
6. Would it bother you to sell something that continues to rise in price?

Keeping in mind Bernard Baruch's comment, "I know of no investor that ever went broke taking a profit," let's explore the results of our test.

If you answered each question with a "no," you can deal with almost any market situation. If your answers were all on the "yes" side of the ledger, you should restrict your savings and investment plans to bank instruments, guaranteed annuities, and government bonds.

Should your answers have been mid-range—call that four "no's"—mutual funds can play a valuable role in building your estate, funding retirement programs, or planning for future tuition bills. However, you may want to avoid the more speculative funds and the new sector funds.

With our short test of market mettle behind us, and some knowledge of pricing and costs, we will move on to headier and more enlightening issues. But keep in mind bulls, bears, and taxes. After fifty years of losing, the life insurers—with variable annuities and variable life—may be the ultimate winners, at least until a new, revised, forever tax bill is passed!

CHAPTER 2

THE FAMILY OF FUNDS
EVOLVES

"You must lose a fly to catch a trout."

George Herbert, 1640

It would be a very strange sight for our angler friend Weeks or his counterparts and associates of the 1930s to pick up *Barron's* or the Sunday *Times* these days. The idea of a mutual fund in those dim and distant ages was quite different from the media message circa 1987.

In the 1930s, the creation of a mutual fund involved a manager of all then-known investment instruments specifically bringing to the marketplace a mutual fund—either blue chip stocks or a balance between stocks and bonds. Often the motivation of these managers of accounts for the wealthy was by necessity rather than greed. The truly wealthy family hired a manager or trustee. That wealthy family was related to others not so rich.

The mutual fund provided the simple facility by which smaller pools of money could be managed economically. "Cousin Charley can hire the rich folks' managers at Scudder now, because they have a mutual fund." Little did they realize that the fund might outperform the private account upon which the rich folks had settled!

In the previous chapter we spoke to the issue of the emerging mutual fund family, and the onset of the major mutual fund development of the 1980s—the variable insurance or universal variable life contract. We noted there what "old hands" know on

Wall Street: "What goes around, comes around." That is, what's new is not really new, but rather is a rehash of something that happened long ago.

"We have reinvented the stock market," say some mutual fund sponsors. Clearly, others have reinvented bonds, and in a way that might truly be called invention: government bonds, long and short; municipal bonds, long, intermediate, short, and insured or not; junk and almost-junk bonds, in varied maturities; zero coupon bonds (bonds that pay no interest right now, but pay off on a "total return" basis at some future date); and so forth. Also, there are bond funds—a term which intuits the feeling of safety—that hedge the safe portfolio of bonds with highly leveraged "puts," "calls," and other intended protective devices. How can one hedge a safe and good thing with a speculative and presumably unsafe thing, and have it still be referred to as "safe"?

THE MARKETS NOW MAJOR IN COMPLEXITY

It seems to us that the markets—the financial malls created by Wall Street and money managers—have become complex at a rate that dwarfs the intellectual and pragmatic wisdom of the potential user. This comment is not meant to discredit the buyer—you—in any way. On an absolute basis, the customer for financial services has learned quite a lot and these days even reads the fine print.

However, the Wall Street and asset-management mill runs roughly as fast as the printing presses creating new, large-denomination greenbacks at the Treasury! Thus, the innovators of things financial—and your present authors were in the front rank of such innovators—are wittingly inventing things that you may or may not need, under a proven assumption that some person, somewhere, will buy almost anything.

REINVENTING THE MARKET

Fidelity Funds *has* reinvented it, Vanguard is trying, and so are Putnam and other asset-management sponsors. A sponsor, in this context, is like the life insurance company or bank with whom you deal. The "fund sponsor" is the entity that hopes to attract your money, offering things that your broker might have offered in years past.

Fidelity has, indeed, reinvented the market of stocks and bonds. Vanguard is not far behind. Putnam, Franklin, Keystone, and others are working on the reinvention. As mutual fund families reinvent the markets—savings, gold bullion, real estate, bonds, stocks—and as each of these is divided into very finite market segments, your choices become both more interesting and more dangerous.

"We Offer 35 Funds In The New Market!"

"Give me any industry and time frame, and I'll give you a winner." There is little doubt that the Fidelity approach is slathered with sales sizzle. In the chapter on strategies, we will deal with the "how-to" of winning with these strange new sector funds.

WHAT GOES AROUND, COMES AROUND

The modern mutual fund family has been around since the 1930s. The fund sponsors that did not recognize the phenomenon or the trends have capitalized mightily on this bull market to reintroduce "old hat" as "new." The keys to it all are found in later chapters. Read on!

A BIT OF HISTORY

Mutual funds with a growth objective are not new. However, prior to the early 1960s there were relatively few growth mutual funds. As we noted in Chapter 1, in the beginning the industry majored in funds that owned blue chip stocks or ran portfolios balanced between stocks and bonds.

Following the long and powerful bull market of the 1950s, growth funds began to emerge in large numbers. The financial press lists hundreds of these today. The small supply of growth funds that existed during that heady market time produced huge capital gains for the modest number of investors who had joined the game early.

Thus we could characterize the mutual funds of that period as being opportunistic. They sat with their blue chip and balanced funds and watched the few growth funds leap to the top of the charts. Then, with media and fund literature supporting great growth examples, they climbed aboard.

However, this departure from the old and proven ways did attract large volumes of money to manage and droves of new investors. The formula of forming new and ever more risky growth funds persisted until the market crash of 1973–74. This event witnessed many of the super growth funds created in the 1960s lose 60 percent or more of their market value! Investors became disenchanted and rushed to the sidelines, licking their fiscal wounds.

However, the funds had now broken out of the mold of the blue chip/balanced-management scenario. Fund sponsors that had one or a few funds were broadening the base. The opportunistic strategy that had worked well in the growth fund boom of the 1960s continued.

The next broadening of the product base came in the early and mid-1970s with the money market mutual fund. Many fund groups formed cash funds or trusts and waited for the money to pour in. But the game had changed in a very important way. The cash funds could not stand the burden of a sales charge.

A few were formed with sales loads. These attracted very little money and were scrapped. Since stock brokers in those days sold most of the mutuals, the idea of offering a no-load money mutual fund was not at all on their minds or in their hearts. "I'll be damned if I'll offer these and not get paid!" was a common outburst at brokerage-house sales meetings. "I don't care how good or useful they are."

However, the family of mutual funds in the stables of many sponsors had expanded another notch. Market and investor psychology would soon make these no-load money funds the darlings of most fund families, and future Wall Street historians will likely refer to these as the tools that brought about today's mutual fund boom.

First, double-digit inflation and soaring interest rates were on the horizon. Since money market mutuals invest in highly liquid short-term investments, they produced current income returns sharply higher than bank instruments. Also, the investments held were almost without risk. Thus they became a proxy for a savings account or bank certificate of deposit, but paid higher interest.

Second, they became progressively more like a bank with the introduction of check writing. Although the check-writing privilege for most funds was restricted to $500 or more, transfer into the funds to earn a few more percentage points was easy. A check could be written to return the funds to the personal or company checking account when needed. This convenience factor, coupled with little risk exposure and higher current returns, attracted billions of dollars of assets into these funds.

The yearning for those higher returns was so great that some employers offered to deposit paychecks to the money funds. After all, during periods of time when checking accounts were paying no interest on deposits, money market mutuals paying double-digit returns and crediting interest daily were very beneficial to employees.

Lastly, entire generations of investors had overstayed the 1960s bull market. Not just the growth mutual fund holders that got clobbered in the 1973–74 big-bear market, but millions of investors in individual stocks were hurt. Fearful of ever-higher inflation and concerned about further market losses, the money market mutual with its apparently huge returns and little risk seemed like nirvana.

Of course, as we will see in later chapters, the actual return earned (money market interest earned, adjusted for taxes and inflation) was inferior to many investment alternatives. But the perceptions of large returns and rapid compounding of those returns attracted savers and investors of all categories. If the word is not the thing, as former Senator Sam Hayakawa would insist, net investment return is no different.

The race to develop new products and expand the sponsor's offerings was off and running. The typical large fund families now consisted of the original blue chip, balanced, and income funds, one or more growth funds created in the 1960s, and one or more money market funds in the following decade.

The typical investor, within the fabric of these expanded offerings with different investment objectives and management styles, could cover most savings and investment bets. The investor could use the cash fund when scared of the market, or when liquidity was needed; the stock, growth, or balanced funds could be used when the investor felt bullish or the investment objective was long-term. There will be more on this subject when we discuss investment-performance-market timing and strategy.

Market events were on the dim horizon that would further expand the now growing mutual fund family. Wall Street was at work creating new investment devices. The long bout with price inflation had literally destroyed the long-term bond market. Inflation had also created a host of folks that believed it would never go away, and who now embrace gold and other precious metals as the salvation for their savings. Many fund groups added precious metals funds to soak up assets from the inflation cult. Other fund groups formed "option-income" funds using new Wall Street tools to hedge against portfolio risks—for example, puts and calls—while producing sharply higher current income returns.

Thus many sponsors of funds had added one or more new choices for their broker and investor following. And, as the 1980s came into view, the expansion was about to become explosive, with funds adding new variations by the bakers dozen. After all, Newton's Law works on Wall Street and in the world economy. Thus what was up would likely be subject to Newton's profound and persuasive gravity.

Those cherished money market fund yields were about to plummet as the era of sustained price inflation gave way to disinflation when the Reagan Presidency took hold. The economy was becoming more global. Cultists of another stripe—against tobacco, South Africa, nuclear energy, defense spending, alcohol—were active in the wings.

As inflation began to diminish apace, Franklin Funds was on stream with a fund that invested only the securities issued by the Government National Mortgage Association. These securities, guaranteed by Uncle Sam, began to yield more to investors than the previous darlings, the money funds. Sure, the risk was a bit larger because these bonds rose or fell in tune with interest rates at large. But "they give me a few percent more, and they're *guaranteed* by the Treasurer of the U.S.!"

The term "Ginnie Mae" became popular. Almost overnight, Franklin's entry became the largest mutual fund in the world. Sponsors were quick to copy this Franklin phenomonon, and today most fund families offer one or many varieties of government bond funds. These government funds have been the most successful new product offerings in the history of the fund industry!

If one recalls the greatest instant fund success of the past— speculative growth funds in the 1960s—and the aftermath, caution is the first word that comes to mind. "If making money were easy," a sage Wall Street hand once observed, "why are there so few rich people and so many with average wealth?"

Since U.S. government-based funds were powering the boom in fund sales, all variety of new bond funds were created. A large segment of the population was being taxed at high rates, and tax shelter sales were booming. Therefore, it is no surprise that tax-free bond funds would pour forth like a river in spate. These, dating back to the late 1950s as closed-end unit trusts, were now available as conventional open-end funds. Most fund sponsors saw the immediate need for one or a bevy of them.

Where the original tax-exempt bond funds and trusts were national in nature, focusing essentially on the larger federal taxes, many groups in the 1980s began to offer these on a state-by-state basis. More than a dozen states with high personal taxes and large taxable populations now have state-dedicated tax-exempt mutuals: New York, California, Ohio, Massachusetts, Pennsylvania, and even little Rhode Island among them.

It is fair to note that much if not all of the innovation by the fund industry has occurred in the recent past or during present market action. New funds tend to be formed after the fact, rather than in anticipation of favorable market trends.

While not the case with the new sector funds, this penchant for the past in new fund offerings can be painful for investors. This retrospection, or twenty-twenty hindsight, tends to attract investment after the bulk of the action has taken place.

HOW LARGE HAS THE FUND GAME BECOME?

As Figure 2–1 illustrates, mutual funds have become a very big business indeed. Considering the continued rise in stock prices, and the continued boom in new sales, it is likely that the industry totals more than $900 billion in assets as we write this.

That near-trillion dollars does not include tax exempt-unit trusts, or the boom in offerings of closed-end stocks or niche funds. If these industry segments were added to the open-ended

FIGURE 2–1
Investment Company Institute Statistics for January 1987

Mutual Fund Monthly Indicators			
	Latest Month	Preceding Month	Year Ago Month
Mutual Funds Statistical Data for January:			
Total Sales of Shares, Mil $	24,857.9	21,578.9	15,087.3
Aggressive Growth	1,203.2	616.5	874.8
Growth	1,763.9	1,186.7	884.8
Growth-and-Income	3,088.5	3,161.2	1,529.6
Precious Metals	124.3	51.9	57.8
International	744.2	657.7	307.5
Balanced	331.3	265.8	268.1
Income	1,546.7	1,049.1	744.2
Option/Income	231.6	219.5	187.4
Government Income	6,059.5	5,576.2	3,856.2
GNMA (Ginnie Mae)	2,513.8	2,329.9	2,071.3
Corporate Bond	2,401.7	2,074.2	1,333.4
Long-Term Municipal Bond	3,035.4	2,870.0	1,861.6
Single State Municipal Bond	1,813.7	1,520.3	1,110.7
Purchases of Common Stocks, Mil $	17,208.2	10,010.5	9,748.9
Sales of Common Stocks	13,437.5	9,222.0	9,319.1
Purchases of Other Securities	37.156.9	35.829.1	22.174.4
Sales of Other Securities	23,792.8	27,315.4	14,443.1
Holdings of Cash & S/T Securities, Mil $	34,522.4	30,716.3	22,424.8
Liquid Asset Ratio (Equity & Balanced)	9.6%	9.5%	9.8%
Total Assets of Funds, Mil $	766,035.7	716,308.0	518,801.2
Money Market	232,710.2	228,345.8	210,615.4
Short-Term Municipal Bond	69,074.8	63,805.8	42,698.4
Stock, Bond, Income Funds	464,250.7	424,156.4	265,487.4
Redemptions of Shares, Mil $	6.883.4	8.922.8	4.554.6

Source: Investment Company Institute Research Dept., Washington, D.C. r-Revised.

fund totals, the industry would surely test the one-trillion asset level, or roughly one-half outstanding federal debt.

Thus, to that earlier, growing fund complex that covered most needs, government, tax exempt, and other types of bond funds were added. To that quality-bond list, where the issuer's credit ranges from perfect to very good, there has been explosive formation of "junk bond" funds. These deal in debt issues where credit is not even a question. Even in the tax-exempt fund area, funds majoring in junk municipal bonds have entered the charge for investor assets. These junk bonds of municipalities and various authorities are not generally considered credit worthy by tested rating services.

Fund groups with ten or more funds have become commonplace rather than rare. In the years when your authors were the senior marketing team at the Keystone Funds (with 12 funds in the mid-1960s), brokers and shareholders commonly complained, "Why do you have so many funds? I have trouble understanding what they are and what purpose they serve."

Global funds investing in foreign securities and funds focused on specific industry sectors became the next major area of innovation. Keystone had a global fund as early as 1954. The early global funds invested world-wide. Funds dealing with specific parts of the world were soon devised as the media began to whip up interest in the huge past-performance numbers. Still other globals were not really global, in the sense that the fund manager might invest some assets in the U.S. as well as abroad.

Early sector funds—those funds that are industry-specific—other than the precious metals variety first made the scene in scientific areas and health care. Families of funds that contained as many as 20 options became more common, and as investors seemed willing to hurriedly fill new fund coffers to the brim, sponsors' drawing boards continued to spew forth new and varied types of funds in record numbers.

However, the growth was not restricted to the old and established fund sponsors. Dozens of new players, observing the rapid growth in assets and those wonderful management fees discussed in Chapter 1, were drawn to the action.

Money managers both new and old joined in at fever pitch. Stock brokers of all size and shape came to play. Venerable and staid casualty insurance companies such as New York's Continental decided that mutual funds were forever, and sponsored a brand-new group. The action today involves all manner of companies, from gas-pipeliner Tenneco to real-estate mogul Southmark Corporation. Each jump in the stock market, further decline in interest rates, or wave of new fund offerings expands the size and variety of fund choices, and explodes the number of sponsors. Many of the new sponsors are at great distances from Wall Street and the venerated traditions that built the mutual fund industry. One asks, "Is the game one of need or greed?"

These families of funds in ever-growing numbers also have ever-increasing stables to offer. Many families are reaching 25 funds or more. Stock and growth funds are reaching for $10 billion in size, and some bond funds are searching for $20 billion in assets.

While the fund sponsor more often identified with the sector area is Fidelity—whose sector funds were illustrated earlier as Figure 1–1—Vanguard has been no slouch in product innovation, sectors included. From its beginnings in 1928 as the Wellington Fund—a conservative, blue chip, total-return fund—the group now boasts 38 funds (the second largest family of funds) with more than its share of specialty products (see Figure 2–2). Included in the Vanguard offerings are index funds. These, using the computer, attempt to match market results in both periods of rising prices and bear markets.

Special funds dealing only with specific sectors of the stock market had, as noted earlier, been a hit-or-miss item until the drawing boards at the Fidelity Funds and Vanguard Group—both long-term fund sponsors—got wind of the action created by the huge bull market in progress. Both of these sponsors, energetic originators of new special-purpose sector funds, took the modern fund family to all-time new highs in terms of numbers of funds offered.

Fidelity, in a recent count, offered more than 80 different investment options for the fund holder. Vanguard has 38 funds and the total is rising as we write. And the Securities & Exchange Commission is deluged with new and varied offerings from these goliaths and other fund sponsors racing to the feed bucket!

FIGURE 2–2
The Vanguard Group

Vanguard Group:					
BdMkt		9.99	9.97	9.98	
Convt	n	u10.83	10.78	10.83+	.03✚
Explorer	n	33.64	33.35	33.64+	.17
ExpIII	n	u24.65	24.07	24.65+	.53
Prmcp	n	53.17	52.11	53.17+	.77
QualDivI	n	18.55	18.33	18.55+	.13
QualDvII	n	9.81	9.75	9.81+	.07
QulDvIII	n	22.85	22.77	22.85+	.08
Quant	n	u12.01	11.60	12.01+	.34
STAR	n	u12.22	12.08	12.22+	.09
TCEF Int	n	43.92	43.36	43.92+	.56✚
TCEF USA	n	u35.38	33.99	35.38+	1.29✚
GNMA	n	10.16	10.12	10.15+	.03
HiY Bond	n	9.42	9.42	9.42	
IG Bond	n	8.76	8.75	8.76+	.01
ShrtTrm	n	10.68	10.67	10.67	
US Tr	n	10.39	10.36	10.37—	.01
IndexTrust	n	u30.02	29.02	30.02+	.83✚
MunHiYd	n	10.96	10.92	10.92—	.04
MuniInt	n	12.58	12.57	12.57—	.01
MuniLong	n	11.39	11.37	11.37—	.01
MuInsLng	n	12.15	12.11	12.11—	.04
MuniShrt	n	15.54	15.53	15.53—	.02
Cal Ins	n	10.64	10.63	10.63	
NYIns	n	10.21	10.17	10.17—	.06
PennI	n	10.47	10.43	10.43—	.04
VSPE	n r	u13.81	13.15	13.81+	.76
VSPGd	n r	u11.93	11.52	11.93+	.49
VSPH	n r	u21.21	20.78	21.21+	.35
VSPS	n r	20.04	19.68	20.04+	.23
VSPT	n r	14.97	14.65	14.97+	.28
Wellesley	n	17.16	17.06	17.16+	.07✚
Wellington	n	u18.17	17.79	18.17+	.33
Windsor	n	16.39	16.08	16.39+	.20
Windsr	II	u14.56	14.32	14.56+	.15
WldInt	n	u11.99	11.91	11.91+	.03
WldUS	n	u12.34	12.07	12.34+	.23

Interesting new ideas and concepts also emerged in the crush to form funds with a difference. IDEX funds were formed by the venerable Pioneer-Western Corporation. These, unlike the giant growth and stock funds, were designed to be closed to new investors when assets under management reached $50–75 million. The idea is that the manager—in this case, the same folks who manage the Janus Fund—will have greater flexibility and presumably an opportunity to manage assets more effectively in terms of results.

Also, The Rightime Fund was formed. Unlike mutual funds that purchase stocks, bonds, and money market instruments, Rightime buys shares of other mutual funds: stock and growth funds when bullish on the market, and cash funds when fearful of a market decline. Thus Rightime management follows the record of other money managers, attempting to own the best of these funds over time while eliminating those with mediocre performance: a timely and interesting idea.

"All things having to do with money," our partner Mike Walsh postulates, "wear out in time!" Even money itself will wear out and be replaced by something else of real value. Thus the absolute and geometric growth in the number and type of available mutuals may be a harbinger of things to come.

These writers, as well as other astute long-term observers of people, money, and greed, and Wall Street at large, have seen great fads come and go. But fads leave the limelight and have led lots of folks to poverty. In one well-worn line: "Bulls make money, bears make money, but pigs go to slaughter." Such, historically, has been the way of sure things and other Wall Street fads.

EVOLUTION, EVOLUTION, EVOLUTION

The primary thing in real estate investment, said the gurus of the early and mid-1980s, was "location, location, location." When inflation eroded and the new tax bill came into being, the best location in Houston or Denver could not save these gurus. Some of the presumedly smartest of them, burdened with debt and shrinking pocketbooks, look less brilliant today. The investors suffered even more.

Will this or something similar occur in the burgeoning mutual fund area? Can disaster strike today's largest and most powerful financial fad? What might occur to blunt the heady growth and frantic innovation? After all, everyone is doing it today, and the stakes are nothing short of gigantic—for the fund sponsors as well as the growing multitudes they serve, or presume to.

LARGE RISKS AND LEVERAGED THINKING

Market sector funds are hardly new. Will growth in families of mutual funds result in a profit for you, or a possible loss? Are these proliferating fund possibilities an advantage or a glaring boondoggle?

First, the mutual fund industry is little different from other competitive businesses. There are economies of scale to be dealt with in funds as there are in producing automobiles or bobby socks. Scale, in this context, relates to the sheer volume of assets under management.

Keen observers gauge that the modern mutual fund needs something more than $100 million to be a profit center; that is, for the money manager to pay all of the bills and have some small sum left over. Without profits, the fund sponsor can lose interest or see the best and brightest managers leave camp for more attractive vistas.

Hundreds of new funds are being formed by novices. These folks may have fine track records. They often manage large scale pension and endowment assets, or large personal fortunes. Some are steeped in Wall Street discipline as investment bankers, underwriters of bonds and stocks, or operators of retail brokerage outlets.

Distribution of mutual funds is big business—expensive business. The competition for the broker's attention is enormous. The enthusiasm for new fund names—particularly when the sponsor is also a new, untested name—wanes as the field gets larger. Thus one might expect than many of these new funds will never reach the break-even point.

Historically, since no fund we know of has actually gone broke—in sharp counterpoint to banks and thrift institutions these days!—the shareholder might expect, at worst, poor management of the assets and skimpy shareholder service. At best—though not really good news—the shareholder might see the brilliant new fund, bought with such heady anticipation of profits, merged with another larger entity.

Thus if mutual fund sales falter, or the field becomes overcrowded, the expectation is for a shakeout among those sponsors who cannot afford the growing costs for distribution and shareholder service. Worse, as the inclination for higher risk is fueled by the media and fund advertising, might be a sharp or protracted bear market for stocks.

History documents that the growth sector of the fund industry attracts the largest sums when the market has been driven to high levels. History again illustrates that these shares, purchased at high prices, are usually sold when the next bear market proves, as always, that the market moves both up and down. No tree grows to the sky. Yet every generation of investors forgets reality and believes that this market is *different*.

Presently the bulk of new fund purchases still focuses on the income and safety areas. U.S. government bond funds, followed by tax-exempt and quality corporate bond funds, dominate the sales charts. Thus the stock market may have much more room to move on the upside.

However, the warning remains intact. The new small funds, particularly when oriented toward growth, speculation, and industry specialization, may have to face the facts of changing market and investor economics as the present bull market concludes.

If we recall that the mutual funds that made it unscathed through the Great Crash in 1929–33 were primarily blue chip owners or balanced funds, we note a sharply higher risk tolerance today. Sector funds, by definition, are speculative.

- In most industries—banking and insurance and public utilities excepted—there are one or a few blue chips, a few growth companies, and a host of lesser firms.
- Market sectors are not likely to move in unison with the stock market itself; i.e., the market averages may rise crisply, but major sectors may lag behind that rise, or decline.

Thus sectors such as computer software and services, transportation, technology, energy, and health care provide little defense in a large or lasting bear market. You will read more about this angle in Chapter 4, where risk and reward are discussed in detail.

Sectors may *appear* to be a simple way to play the market; however, if the wrong sectors are selected, the investor may miss major profit opportunities. One of the key reasons for purchasing mutual funds is professional management. A key in that management process is to weight the broadly diversified portfolio of holdings in favor of better-performing groups while reducing or eliminating assets invested in segments that perform less well.

On the flip side of the sector fund question, numerous advisory services have been formed in an attempt to bring order and advice to the confused buyer audience. These have yet to be tested over full market cycles. However, one or more may emerge as great sector pickers.

Keep in mind that use of one or more of these services, which are fee-based, will increase the cost of ownership, and therefore reduce total investment returns. Are they worth using? Time will tell.

To exacerbate the increasing leverage in the mutual fund area, particularly at large and sector funds, is the move by Fidelity—certainly to be copied by other sponsors if successful—to offer a short-selling plan.

A short sale of securities is made when shares are borrowed and sold. These shares are to be replaced at some future time. The speculator (the short seller in this case) is betting that the price will decline enough to cover the cost of borrowing and still produce a profit. Fidelity Funds is introducing the short-sale program for its "Select" or sector funds. Thus the most speculative aspects of stock trading are being introduced to the fund industry.

As the market moves ever upward, investors of the safe and saving variety, and the blue chip buyers, will begin looking for the quick profit. The proliferation of new funds coupled with new methods of speculating in funds can, in our view, only lead to trouble. Trouble, where Wall Street is concerned, generally is a code word for losses.

AND NOW FOR THE GOOD NEWS!

Creativity and innovation in the modern mutual fund family are not restricted to new funds or products. The computer is also doing its thing. The way funds report to shareholders and their advisors is taking a new shape. For example, if the shareholder owns three different funds in a family, should three statements be mailed, or one?

A small Boston group, International Heritage Fund, offering five asset-allocation options, delivers both the shareholder and the broker a consolidated statement. Thus, to keep up with taxes or merely count up the chips at month's end, one statement rather than three is indeed a major improvement. We expect more of this as shareholders and brokers demand more in return for the ever-increasing costs of management discussed in Chapter 1.

Also, as readers will see in the chapter covering asset allocation, the recently formed Sass*Southmark funds make computer software available to brokers and planners that brings a high level of sophistication to the serious questions: What do I want my money to earn, and how do I allocate the assets available to reduce market risk and enhance investment reward? We expect a stream of software development by fund groups to help unravel investor questions in light of the thousands of fund choices available.

Can charge cards using mutual fund assets be far away? We think not. Chapter 11 will deal with funds and fund services in the future in some detail. For the moment, as we move into the major issue in fund selection—performance measurement—one final word is warranted: caution.

There are many, many funds. There is a growing penchant to buy newness and smallness. There is a built-in desire to own best performance, and in bull markets that leads to increasingly speculative choices. Caution is a great word to remember when the fund-selection game becomes one of looking for the quick turn, the instant profit.

Performance—total return earned from investing—is the subject of Chapter 3. As a primer, ponder this analogy. For the previous ten years, you were correct in deciding if the stock market would do better than bonds, or the reverse, that bonds would outperform stocks. However, you were a terrible stock picker, always in the worst performing group. And, you were no better in bonds. Thus you were a perfect picker of markets, but a terrible picker of individual issues and bond maturities. (When purchasing a mutual fund, those attributes—picking markets and selecting the correct issues—are among the most important to look for in a fund manager.)

How did you come out as a good picker of markets and a poor picker of stocks?

- Measured against the universe of top money managers you stood in the top 3 percent . . . that is, you did as well or better than 97 percent of the field.
- Measured against the bond manager universe, your result was in the top 1 percent!

Thus, while you were wrong in an element of the process often assigned the highest marks, you in fact bested the system in a very substantial way. After all, for a mutual fund or manager to be in the top 25 percent of all managers with consistency will over time produce the number one result. We will cover these performance and evaluation questions as we move to Chapter 3.

As one observer of the scene notes, "Economics was designed to give astrology a good name." Liars figure, and figures lie. Now, on to the world of figures and economics.

CHAPTER 3

RESULTS, RESULTS, RESULTS: MUTUAL FUND PERFORMANCE

"A study of economics usually reveals that the best time to buy anything is last year."

Marty Allen, 1972

Even the *Ladies Home Journal* does it these days. It does, that is, a quarterly review of mutual fund performance, with heady copy on who is best and who was the winner for a string of prior market periods.

This phenomenon—quarterly sections filled with fund income and performance data—once was the domain of market watchers such as *Barron's Weekly* and *Forbes*, respected market publications. Today no self-respecting editor misses the opportunity to review fund results for readers.

And, to make matters more complex for potential or existing fund investors, subscription advisory services are springing up in droves. They range from generalist publications such as the *Mutual Fund Forecaster* out of Fort Lauderdale, to specific fund-group coverage by *O'Malley's Fidelity Watch* based in Ellisville, Missouri, and they not only discuss track records but also engage in price and market-sector prediction.

Thus we have a vast body of print copy discussing the past. These documents resemble quarterly history books loaded with facts, statistics, and fictions. These history lessons cost a few bucks apiece. If the reader needs more, the fund advisory services range in price from one hundred to more than a few hundred dollars.

To add to this data glut, we quote Fidelity Funds' *New York Times* full-page advertisement on February 22, 1987: "Confused About 1,122 Funds?" In addition to the print media, we are assured that major mutual fund sponsors will be pleased to pass along reams of illustrations documenting the answer to that ever present question, "Who's Best?"

In reviewing a series of quarterly fund results updates, and attempting to find some merit in either the plethora of new advisories or the overwhelming amount of fund advertising, the authors are reminded that you simply cannot buy yesterday's results. In particular, you cannot buy them where stock, growth, and the new sector or niche funds are concerned. Where investments involving a lot of price volatility are the issue, yesterday is indeed just that: history! Yet you can buy mutual fund performance histories by the pound—for money—at most newsstands these days.

QUALITY REPORTING?

A history book written by a noted member of academe about a time, event, or personage is typically documented to the teeth. References to other esteemed works on the same or a similar topic abound. Facts and theories presented painstakingly by the author either render the history as usable, interesting, or a prized bookshelf addition. We think of Winston Churchill's *A History of the English Speaking People* as a fine example of fact and theory blended into readable and thoughtful history, or Edward A. Weeks' *Writers and Friends* as a study of authors' craftmanship and editors' observation of those authors.

A review of *Barron's, Money, Business Week*, and other mutual fund performance histories, quarter by quarter, reveals little that would generate a passing grade in any major university history department! In basketball a lay-up or a free throw is a "gimme." With the modern computer, networking by modem or press service, and simple use of the telephone and logic, one might conclude that staid financial publications will have accurate data and report that data as a historic reality. Readers who believe that would be in error!

First, there appear to be glaring oversights. For example, even *Barron's*—The "National Business and Financial Weekly" for sixty-seven years!—does not always have the facts. Capital-gains distributions are sometimes omitted even months after being paid. Dividends from income are sometimes not reported at all, or are well behind the payment cycle. If *Barron's*—the originator of the quarterly and weekly fund-history game, and sister to the venerated *Wall Street Journal*—cannot get the numbers right, then who can?

Yet millions of Americans—particularly the do-it-yourself buyer—invest and save billions of dollars based on the printed facts . . . or the articulation that inevitably accompanies those presumed facts. However, a missing dividend here or there does not convict or besmirch the financial press at large. What may is the nature and style of the related reporting, and the quickness of fund sponsor printing press power when their fund is ranked number one!

So the numbers are not quite up to snuff. So what? Any decent mutual fund management—and most of these folks are decent—will correct any discrepancies over the phone on their toll-free number, or by mail with a copy of the latest quarterly or annual report and a prospectus. These well-meaning people sometimes even believe that the investor reads these documents and understands the complex accounting. Many fund sponsors will also "crunch some numbers" for the caller that will fix the reporting period to the actual needs of the saver or investor; for instance, no one invests on the first business day of January, or sells on the subsequent final trading day of December . . . or five, ten or fifteen years later, for that matter.

The larger issue is one related to understanding. The reader purchasing *Barron's* or *Money* magazine expects that the few bucks of cash outlay buys accurate and prescient advice and fund-knowledgeable commentary. To say that this assumption is in error might be the understatement of our times. . .like Boesky saying he never met anyone from Drexel Burnham or Kidder Peabody!

For example, one quarterly review of mutual fund results—the first published by this important business publication—commented that in the final quarter of the year mutual funds raised cash for purposes of "window-dressing." Window-dressing is Wall Street jargon for making the portfolio that will be reported to the fund shareholder contain those stocks which have done well in price in previous months. In other words, dress up the portfolio with recent winners. Millions of readers, we assume, believed this fallacy! With the above pronouncement in mind, one author wrote to the magazine's editor about the mistaken identity of "window dressing".

- Since the fiscal year-end for reporting purposes often is December 31, the fund manager must raise cash to cover distributions to holders that are scheduled in early January.
- Many mutual funds, such as sector or fully invested funds, simply cannot window-dress since the hot-performing stocks or stock groups do not qualify for ownership by the fund.
- The fund has a large constituency in the pension area. Cash demands will be large since the actuarial age of the large pension plan is going to require substantial cash outlay.
- A major investor in the fund has announced to management that liquidation will occur soon; thus cash must be raised. This is particularly true if the fund has a market-timing following, a subject we will discuss in detail in later chapters.
- The manager, looking at upcoming new offerings of bonds or stocks in January, is raising cash to cover the cost of purchase. . .to which the manager is committed!
- The manager has opted to alter strategy—in the market of late, that might mean moving from foreign investments to domestic.

To merely call all cash-balance or liquid-asset increases "window-dressing" is to generalize to the natural level of stupidity. Yet millions of Americans will read and believe what they read.

Since each fund has a specific, printed investment objective, the manager will operate the fund on that basis. But managers of mutual funds do change jobs. Is it "Fidelity" or is it the named "manager" that we depend on? We believe the latter—the fund manager—is more important, other things being equal. Who makes the investment result? Is it Dreyfus, or Vanguard, or T. Rowe Price; or is it the human beings who make daily decisions on behalf of the army of investors who use that fund for need or greed satisfaction? The authors believe that the genuine history of a mutual fund's performance—the total return to the investor that equals the capital gains paid on profits actually earned—will be written not by the fund itself, but by the adroit portfolio manager who calls the market-, stock-, and industry-selection shots with better than median correctness. Thus the fund or fund group is really nothing more or less than a name. The managers and analysts are everything!

Quarterly reports in *Barron's* and other financial publications, ranking the human managers, and tracking their employment changes, are where the meat of investment history and future lies. A sincere improvement in reporting the numbers would be quite useful, since historic performance is indeed meaningful if reported in a proper format (more on that as we move along). And financial writers at work on these quarterly performance escapades would do well to understand what a mutual fund is, how it works and is managed, and learn how to describe the process to serious investors and savers actually risking their money! Figure 3–1 shows a performance illustration typical of those provided to customers by brokerage houses.

THE PROGNOSTICATORS

There is diagnosis and prognosis. Diagnosis relates to the known, where prognosis deals with the future. The aforementioned quarterly histories engage in diagnosis. Here is the ill or pain; it is diagnosed as being good performance or bad. Prognosis is more interesting and, indeed, more important, since the past is clearly history—you cannot buy it because it has already occurred. Yet, unfortunately, most investors do focus on buying the past.

A great example of buying the past versus the future can be found in the stock market crash of 1973–74. Keystone S–4, a fully invested stock fund with terrific price volatility, was a

FIGURE 3–1
Performance Diagnosis—A.G. Edwards

Fund Size (Millions)	Growth Funds	Total Return				
		1986	1985	5 Years	10 Years	15 Years
$ 6.9	Fidelity Destiny II	+60.45%	N/A	—	—	—
242.5	Phoenix Growth	+19.24	+31.84	+218.04%	+531.55%	+ 578.36%
1,074.2	Fidelity Destiny I	+18.60	+29.06	+203.06	+613.79	+1,038.21
740.7	Growth Fund of America	+16.23	+27.08	+122.17	+590.08	+ 404.59
230.1	Keystone S-3	+16.19	+23.20	+103.37	+270.28	+ 275.21
1,384.8	AMCAP	+15.54	+16.87	+116.22	+533.99	+ 578.31
273.7	Kemper Summit	+14.75	+27.47	+113.37	+482.53	+ 519.20
76.5	Security Action Plan	+13.54	+29.36	+108.89	—	—
275.1	Kemper Growth	+13.41	+14.09	+115.68	+361.15	+ 436.13
719.3	New Economy	+13.26	+36.86	—	—	—
64.6	American Growth	+ 6.39	+13.52	+ 79.14	+303.73	+ 406.58
542.6	Keystone S-4	+ 6.00	+28.24	+ 59.46	+279.84	+ 159.43
858.4	Mass. Capital Development	+ 5.73	+18.41	+109.25	+581.64	+ 518.20
	Averages	+16.87%	+24.67%	+122.60%	+454.85%	+ 491.42%
	Dow Jones Ind. Average	+27.25%	+27.66	+176.28	+222.43	+ 350.12
	Standard & Poor's 500	+18.67	+26.33	+147.67	+266.46	+ 364.95

	Latest Available		Return on Initial $10,000 Investment			
	Price/ Earnings	Annual % Turnover	1 Year*	5 Years*	10 Years*	15 Years*
Fidelity Destiny II	N/A	N/A	—	—	—	—
Phoenix Growth	18.5	151%	$11,029	$29,418	$58,418	$62,748
Fidelity Destiny I	16.5	86	—	—	—	—
Growth Fund of America	36.0	24	10,635	20,328	63,142	46,169
Keystone S-3	23.5	137	10,631	18,608	33,880	37,521
AMCAP	25.2	27	10,571	19,784	58,010	62,065
Kemper Summit	22.8	60	10,614	19,736	53,884	57,276
Security Action Plan	N/A	90	—	—	—	—
Kemper Growth	21.8	97	10,490	19,950	42,656	49,592
New Economy	32.3	22	10,363	—	—	—
American Growth	21.4	58	9,841	16,570	37,345	46,732
Keystone S-4	32.1	83	10,600	15,946	37,984	25,943
Mass. Capital Development	26.0	117	9,832	19,460	63,392	57,492
Averages			$10,460	$19,977	$49,856	$49,504
Dow Jones Ind. Average			$12,725	$27,628	$32,243	$45,012
Standard & Poor's 500			11,867	24,767	36,646	46,495

big seller in the early 1970s. Much of the sales muscle came from heady prior performance as reported in *Barron's* and other print media.

When the bottom of the powerful decline was reached in late fall 1974, the fund was down almost 70 percent from the net asset value recorded in December of 1972. The investors buying on the basis of past performance at the high price had largely sold their shares on the way down, sustaining large losses. Buying the past, in this case, was tantamount to disaster. To make matters even worse, many buyers of the fund were not aware that:

1. The stock fund was fully invested in stocks at all times and could not take defensive measures, and
2. The type of company owned by Keystone S–4 tends to be among the most risky; that is, subject to the largest decline in bear markets.

THE R AND X FACTORS

Another argument vis à vis past performance are the "R" and "X" factors. Lipper Advisors is a premier scorekeeper for the mutual fund industry. Much of the data used by the financial press for quarterly fund reporting is assembled by Lipper. These reports now footnote a growing number of "Rs"—a redemption fee may apply—or, more disconcerting, "Xs"—the fund is closed to new accounts.

The Lipper study of results for five time periods ending 12/31/86 contains 23 such footnotes for the 25 top performers in each category. That is, 11 had added a redemption fee, and 12 were closed to new investors. In almost 10 percent of the group, the investment merit either has been affected by an exit fee, or the shares cannot be purchased no matter how attractive the record or prospects!

Let's summarize the past price action derby with a key point:

Most of last year's big performance winners will likely become tomorrow's losers! That is a historic fact.

Looking at the advertising in the print media, diagnosis and prognosis become the same word. The major fund advertisers almost always buy the largest amount of space to promote *last year's* big winner. In late 1986 and early 1987, that often meant the "global," "overseas," "foreign," or "world" funds.

Obviously the world is coming together. Equally thoughtful and logical is the idea that investment moneys in a contracting world buffeted by monetary and economic forces can create solid total returns which might exceed those being earned in the U.S. markets. That is true, the idea worked, and the concept—big gains in non-U.S. stocks—has already happened!

But the fund managements in this area budgeted heavily to capture new investors for last year's winning idea. These folks did not buy full-page spreads three or four years ago to tout the idea. They waited until the record numbers materialized, and then they went to press.

With much of the advertising focused on foreign stock funds, and fund sponsors introducing new global funds apace, we find the bull market in our domestic markets interesting. *Barron's* provides a neat table each week that compares the U.S. market to all other "major" markets. In the issue dated February 23, 1987, *Barron's'* "Global Stock Markets" notes that the world market rose 1.6 percent for the week. The U.S. market rose 3.5 percent outdistanced only by those in Spain and Norway.

- Of the 20 markets reported, seven reported net declines in value when translated to U.S. Dollars.
- Three more markets delivered increases smaller than 1 percent on the same basis.
- The U.S. exchanges, and funds invested in those stocks, performed at least 120 percent better than the foreign markets.
- And Spain and Norway, both wonderful places to visit, and both capable of producing *Salmo salar* for the angler, are markets that might equal, in dollar magnitude, a small regional exchange here!

Yet "global" is a hot Wall Street and mutual fund word, so roll the presses! Unhappiness is buying the wonderful investment two years or so after the happening. The fund sponsors, always in the business of raising new money for open-end mutual funds, seem to forget this truth when allocating advertising budgets or creating new investment alternatives for the public.

DIAGNOSIS & PROGNOSIS

If the diagnosis is sometimes flawed, should the media and advertising sponsors be subject to malpractice claims? Likely not, since you paid your few bucks, and investment advice and reporting is what it is . . . take it or leave it!

However, while scorekeeping of mutual fund results has been around for decades—Johnson's Charts and Wiesenberger Reports being in the ancient and honorable column—today we observe a major extension in the prognosis area—folks who predict what will occur, not what has occurred.

Boston's United Business Service has been creating timely prognoses for decades, and of late is producing some of the genuinely critical data, such as the funds' Alpha and Beta, which will be dealt with in detail elsewhere in the text.

But today, with more mutual funds than stocks on the "Big Board," and the increasing interest in specialty, sector, niche, industry, country, area, and other esoteric funds, the prognosis game is becoming very big business.

How many investors deal in the commodity markets: gold, or farm produce, for example? There are, we are told, at least 500 fee advisories selling daily, weekly, or other-interval services to that small community. Mutual fund investors certainly top thirty million folks these days. The potential for publishing boggles the imagination. Thus, in recent days, in addition to a host of new mutual funds—estimated at one per business day in 1987–88—the investment landscape is alive with services, for a fee, that will attempt to forecast tomorrow for today's investors.

- Will small funds outperform large funds?
- Will the utility sector continue to perform well relative to the energy or high-tech sector?

- Can quality bond funds continue to deliver double-digit total returns, or should the money shift to stock or growth funds?
- And, which fund managements have the correct idea about tomorrow?

A dozen more questions could be asked, and will be. A dozen more answers are in the hopper. As H. L. Mencken once noted, "I make my statistics up as I go along, 'cause it provides me with innocent amusement!"

Most of the fee-based prognosticators have been around for a day, weeks, or a precious few months. These good folks are capitalizing on a major trend—more fund investors, multiplying choices, increasing complexity. People will need and pay hard dollars for advice.

Advisories focused on the market or interest-rate trends have been around forever, at least for today's investors. Since World War II is long forgotten, we are reminded that Bank Credit Analyst, Lowry Reports, and others have been publishing market and credit advisories regularly since before that time.

But they all follow trends. Today's prognosticators deal with wholly different issues. Unlike Bank Credit Analyst or Lowry's, these subscription services wish to enlighten the investor on such majestic issues as which fund, by type or class, will really produce substantial returns, and which will not! Or, which market segment will be hot or not in the year to come? Figure 3–2 illustrates typical reporting and recommendations that the investor in mutuals can buy these days.

SCHOOL'S OUT!

If investing your hard-earned money were easy, everyone would be doing it and winning. "If," as some sage observer noted, "picking the winners were that easy, the publishing types would be winning with their own money, not soliciting subscriptions!" There is more than a modicum of merit in that remark. We will be privy to the actual results when the huge new Gabelli and

Zweig funds run through a full market cycle. Because today, we are again witness to the cult of Wall Street known as the "star system." A star identification in the 1960s would equate with Gerry Tsai. Today it might be Mario Gabelli or Doctor Martin Zweig. As we have attempted to remind readers throughout, the name is not the thing. Only the total return on investment counts. To put that thought in proper perspective, read the following aloud:

- "If I invested, and as a result owe Uncle Sam a tax payment, I have won."
- "If I invested, and use the transaction as a 'tax loss,' I have lost!"

That is, win or lose, the ultimate investment equation. When we deal later with specific investment strategies, we hope to position you, the reader, to enter the charmed winner's circle.

In the interim, the new mutual fund predictors require time to discover. We assume that all of these are well-meaning, and that some may have merit merely as recorders of our changing times. However, the game—for investments and fund investments—is ever-changing. These services have yet to be tested in the real world of results. We give each one "A" for effort, and at least "B" for timeliness and creativity. But to pick a winner now is impossible.

THE REAL THING

If the newspaper is not always correct, and the quarterly reporting of fund results imperfect, and the subscription advisories too new, and the copy that fund sponsors blast at us speaks to self-interest, then what can we count on as fact in the burgeoning world of mutual funds and mutual fund families?

The answer is found in two words: *consistency*, and *realism!*

- Does the mutual fund family offer multiple-choice answers, or does one fund stand alone as witness to investment prowess?

FIGURE 3-2

Mutual Fund Forecaster (Directory of Mutual Funds: Profit Projections and Risk Ratings)

Current Advice	Mutual Fund	One Year Profit Projection	Risk Rating	Past Performance 1986 (12/31/85-12/31/86)	Past Performance 1985 (12/31/84-12/31/85)	Past Performance 6 Years (12/31/80-12/31/86)	IRA	Keogh	Tele. Switch	Auto. Withdrawal	Telephone (800 = toll free)	State	# States Registered	Minimum Initial Investment	Sales Load	Redemp- tion Fee	Hidden Load
Hold	AARP Capital Growth	+28%	Low	+16%	NA	NA	x	x	x	x	800-253-2277	MA	50	$250			
Best Buy	AARP Growth and Income	+30%	Very Low	+19%	NA	NA	x	x	x	x	800-253-2277	MA	50	250			
Buy	ABT Midwest Emerging Gwth	+36%	Very High	+13%	+44%		x	x	x	x	800-354-0436	OH	50	1,000	9.3%		0.25%
	ABT Midwest Growth & Incm	+30%	Medium	+17%	+33%	+81%	x	x	x	x	800-354-0436	OH	50	1,000	9.3%		0.25%
	ABT Midwest Utility Incm	+30%	Medium	+15%	+23%	NA	x	x	x	x	800-354-0436	OH	50	1,000	9.3%		0.25%
Hold	Acorn Fund	+27%	Very Low	+17%	+32%	+119%	x	x	x	x	312-621-0630	IL	41	1,000			
	Adams Express	+30%	Medium	+21%	+30%	+168%	x	x			Closed-End NYSE 1% Discount					2.0%	
	AFuture	+16%	Very High	−6%	+22%	+30%			x	x	800-523-7594	PA	32	500			
	AIM - Charter	+27%	High	+16%	+26%	+93%	x		x	x	800-231-0803	TX	46	2,000	5.0%		0.30%
Buy	AIM - Constellation Grwth	+37%	Very High	+29%	+29%	+65%	x		x	x	800-231-0803	TX	33	1,000	5.0%		
Buy	Aim - Convertible Yield	+17%	Very Low	+4%	+22%	+69%	x	x	x	x	800-231-0803	TX	45	1,250	5.0%		
	Aim - Weingarten Equity	+38%	Very High	+25%	+36%	+135%	x	x	x	x	800-231-0803	TX	43	1,000	5.0%		0.25%
	Alliance Chemical	+28%	High	+13%	+32%	+78%	x	x	x	x	800-221-5672	NY	50	500	9.3%		
	Alliance Surveyor	+27%	High	+14%	+29%	+58%	x	x	x	x	800-221-5672	NY	50	250	9.3%		
	Alliance Technology	+31%	Very High	+12%	+26%	NA	x	x	x	x	800-221-5672	NY	50	1,000	9.3%		
	AMA - Growth	+28%	High	+11%	+24%	+72%	x	x	x	x	800-523-0864	PA	46	300			0.50%
	AMA - Medical Technology		Very High	+15%	+39%	+84%	x	x	x	x	800-523-0864	PA	46	500			0.50%
	American - AMCAP	+27%	Medium	+15%	+22%	+129%	x	x	x	x	800-421-9900	CA	50	1,000	9.3%		
	American - American MUTL	+29%	Low	+19%	+31%	+187%	x	x	x	x	800-421-9900	CA	50	250	9.3%		
	American - Balanced	+26%	Very Low	+17%	+29%	+159%	x	x	x	x	800-421-9900	CA	50	500	9.3%		
Hold	American - Fundamentl Inv	+34%	Medium	+22%	+29%	+177%	x	x	x	x	800-421-9900	CA	50	250	9.3%		
	American - Growth FD Amer	+30%	Medium	+16%	+27%	+210%	x	x	x	x	800-421-9900	CA	50	1,000	9.3%		
Hold	American - Income FD Amer	+24%	Very Low	+15%	+28%	+200%	x	x	x	x	800-421-9900	NY	50	1,000	9.3%		
Hold	American - Invest CO Amer	+31%	Medium	+19%	+33%	+175%	x	x	x	x	800-421-9900	CA	50	250	9.3%		
Hold	American - New Economy		Medium	+13%	+40%	NA	x	x	x	x	800-421-9900	CA	50	1,000	9.3%		
Hold	American - Washington MUT	+34%	Medium	+21%	+32%	+218%	x	x	x	x	800-421-9900	CA	50	250	9.3%		
	American Capital Comstock	+25%	Low	+13%	+21%	+151%	x			x	713-993-0500	TX	50	500	9.3%		
	American Capital Convrtbl	+23%	Medium	+31%	+18%	+275%					Closed-End NYSE 15% Premium						
	American Capital Enterprs	+30%	High	+10%	+30%	+67%	x			x	713-993-0500	TX	50	00	9.3%		
Hold	American Capital FND Amer	+25%	Low	+6%	+16%	+131%	x			x	713-993-0500	TX	50	500	9.3%		

Rec	Fund		Risk										Phone	State				
	American Capital Harbor	+24%	Very Low	+14%	+24%	+133%						x	713-993-0500	TX	50	500	9.3%	
	American Capital Pace	+26%	Medium	+11%	+22%	+182%						x	713-993-0500	TX	50	500	9.3%	
	American Capital Providnt	+22%	Very Low	+12%	+18%	+164%						x	713-993-0500	TX	49	500	7.8%	
	American Capital Venture	+22%	Very High	+4%	+13%	+114%						x	713-993-0500	TX	48	500	9.3%	
	American Capital OTC	+15%	Very High	-10%	+24%	NA						x	800-421-5666	CA	50	500	9.3%	
	American Investors	+16%	Very High	-2%	+14%	-30%	x					x	800-243-5353	CO	50	400		
	American National Growth	+26%	Very High	+11%	+31%	+120%	x					x	800-231-4639	TX	50	20	9.3%	
	Americna National Income	+24%	Low	+7%	+28%	+152%	x					x	800-231-4639	TX	49	100	9.3%	
Hold	AMEV Capital	+33%	Medium	+22%	+31%	+166%	x					x	800-328-4891	MN	50	25	9.3%	
Buy	AMEV Growth	+33%	High	+20%	+35%	+150%	x					x	800-328-1064	MN	50	250	9.3%	
	Analytic Opt'ioned Equity	+21%	Very Low	+10%	+17%	NA	x					x	714-833-0294	CA	38	25,000		
	Armstrong Associates	+18%	High	+12%	+21%	NA	x					x	214-744-5558	TX	5	250		
	AXE-Houghton Fund B	+27%	Very Low	+23%	+33%	+141%	x	x	x			x	800-431-1030	NY	49	1,000		0.45%
	AXE-Houghton Stock	+30%	Very High	+10%	+31%	+83%	x	x	x			x	800-431-1030	NY	49	1,000		0.45%
Hold	Babson Enterprise	+28%	Low	+9%	+39%	NA	x	x	x			x	800-422-2766	MO	50	1,000		
	Babson Growth	+30%	Medium	+20%	+30%	+96%	x	x				x	800-422-2766	MO	49	500		
Hold	Baker Fentress	+27%	High	+12%	+37%	+193%							Closed-End OTC 14% Discount					
	Bancroft Convertible	+22%	Medium	+18%	+35%	+158%	x					x	Closed-End AMEX 1% Premium					
	Bartlett Basic Value	+16%	Very Low	+13%	+25%	NA	x	x				x	800-543-8721	OH	23	1,000		
	Beacon Hill Mutual	+27%	Medium	+6%	+34%	+97%	x					x	617-482-0795	MA	15	0		
	Berger - One Hundred	+25%	High	+20%	+26%	+57%	x	x	x			x	303-837-1020	CO	25	250		0.30%
Hold	Berger - One Hundred One	+28%	Very Low	+15%	+29%	+135%	x	x	x			x	303-837-1020	CO	21	250		0.30%
Best Buy	Boston CO Capital Apprec.	+33%	Low	+22%	+35%	+140%	x	x	x			x	800-343-6324	MA	50	1,000		0.45%
	Boston CO Special Growth	+21%	High	+7%	+35%	NA	x	x	x			x	800-343-6324	MA	50	1,000		0.45%
Hold	Bruce	+31%	Medium	+30%	+39%	NA						x	312-236-9160	IL	7	1,000		
	Bull-Bear Capital Growth	+24%	High	+4%	+28%	+43%	x	x	x	x		x	800-847-4200	NY	47	1,000		1.00%
	Bull-Bear Equity Income	+23%	Very Low	+19%	+26%	+98%	x	x	x	x		x	800-847-4200	NY	43	1,000		1.00%
	Calvert Equity	+23%	High	+12%	+24%	NA	x	x	x	x		x	800-368-2748	MD	50	2,000		0.75%
	Calvert Social: Mngd Grth	+23%	Very Low	+16%	+24%	NA	x	x	x	x		x	800-368-2748	MD	50	1,000	4.7%	0.50%
	Calvin Bullock - Div Shrs	+33%	Medium	+22%	+31%	+159%	x	x	x	x		x	800-221-5757	NY	50	500	9.3%	
Hold	Calvin Bullock - Growth	+29%	Medium	+16%	+27%	+106%	x	x				x	800-221-5757	NY	50	500	9.3%	
Hold	Castle Convertible	+16%	High	+12%	+11%	+219%	x					x	Closed-End Amex 0% Discount					
Buy	Central Securities	+28%	High	+16%	+22%	+187%	x					x	Closed-End Amex 7% Discount					
	Century Shares	+35%	Medium	+10%	+43%	+192%	x					x	800-321-1928	MA	50	500		
	Cigna Growth	+28%	Medium	+13%	+28%	+95%	x	x				x	203-726-6000	CT	50	500	5.3%	0.20%

Source: The Institute for Econometric Research. Reprinted with permission.

- Has the fund—bond, income, balanced, stock, or growth—been around? Has the management lived in both good and bad times?
- Have investment results been reasonably consistent? In how many full market cycles have the funds performed well when related to all competitors?

An additional point should be made when the word "competitor" comes up. One of the writers was asked once to describe the mutual fund industry to a jury in federal court during a break in a trial. The judge suggested that Wall Street terms be avoided. He asked that the industry be likened to a fruit stand.

Grapefruit were bond funds, lemons were speculative growth funds. The market had just traversed the major decline mentioned a few pages ago, and blue chip stock funds were oranges. Balanced funds were described as nectarines, and the few specialty funds at that time were tangerines.

There is a very important message for investors comparing past price performance, a message lost in today's media reporting: *compare apples with apples.* The top 25 performers highlighted in the Lipper year-end study included all of the above fruit except the grapefruit. If income is your objective, compare a dozen income funds, not a few income funds with a few international or growth funds.

The characteristics of funds change by type of fund and stated objective in the prospectus. Just because a fund is broadly diversified and managed by very capable people does not mean that it will resist market declines. The key elements—asset allocation and risk threshold—will be discussed in the next two chapters.

Think about it for a moment, before you plunk down those dollars for a periodical, or hundreds for an advisory subscription. In salmon fishing, it takes some thousand casts over a known fish before it takes the fly. Yet the flybox is the same for salmon fishing as for investing: thousands of funds, hundreds of weather constraints, differing global weather conditions, and the score to be recorded later, not right away! Mutual funds are the flybox in the investor and saver world. The choices are too numerous to tally. The options indeed boggle even the full-time observer. Where and when—as with the strike of the salmon—will profit occur?

The authors admire the tenacity and sometimes vulgarity of the prognosticators. However, the best idea for readers is to determine which family of funds has recorded exemplary investment results in a variety of areas over many market cycles. American Funds, Kemper, Putnam, Fidelity, Vanguard, T. Rowe Price, Janus, Phoenix, and others shine!

WELL ... WHO DO YOU BELIEVE?

The mutual funds themselves publish some remarkable literature. When asked, they can provide you with telling statistics that relate to the real world.

The funds represent a wholly vested interest. Yet they must comply with securities regulations. So these statistical comparisons—unlike the dividend projections generated by life insurance companies—will tell the whole truth. But you cannot ask merely for a fund illustration. You must ask for information about a specific investment and obtain print tabulations for that fund, or for a combination if requested. More data on this subject will surface when you read the chapters on asset allocation, market timing, risk and reward, and investment strategy.

Be reminded that the past is over, it is history. A mutual fund insurance/investment product—even the new variable life insurance products—is not a guaranteed or certified quantity. Actuarially, the investor can make only guesses, some good and some bad, about forward or prospective total returns. Banks can make guarantees for the short range, a few years or so. However, it appears that banks and their savings sisters were going broke in 1986 at about the same rate—one each day—that new mutual funds were commencing operation!

Life insurance companies also make guarantees when serving up statistical illustrations. These lengthy "numbers crunches" from legal reserve and mutual insurers tend toward long-term assurances. However, the assurances have built-in difficulties in the real world, because the insurers are no better than the government, periodicals, or brokerages in predictive skills. Can they, the insurance companies, tell you what interest rates and inflation will be, and guarantee the result? Of course not. Can the insurers ensure that they will have the reserves available to pay all claims when due? It seems that some could not in recent years. And the reliability of the many insurers that hold portfolios of junk bonds may be questionable.

PERFORMANCE: FOLLOW THE MANAGER

We believe that the great mutual funds tend to perpetuate their greatness. Their success and managerial prowess give them a reputation and visibility that make it possible to attract, hire, and retain the good people who can continue their traditions of achievement.

Many graduates of our best business schools want to work at Salomon Brothers, Morgan Stanley, First Boston, or Goldman Sachs. And there is a trickle-down effect at work, so that some of the finest matriculate at other Wall Street firms.

Fidelity, Putnam, American Funds—among others—are consistent winners because they attract quality people with growth mind-sets. Smaller or less well-known managers—such as Janus, Evergreen, or Phoenix—attract either more entrepreneurial men and women, or those who seek smaller and more relaxed workplaces.

Our experience tells us that the great funds—those with consistency of performance over many, many market cycles—continue to be great because of philosophical and operational disciplines that work, and the ability to attract the very brightest young people. These funds get the best graduate students from the finest universities. They also attract proven managers from Wall Street investment banks and from the bank and trust community as well.

Good examples abound of new funds with quality, proven asset management. Janus, with a superb record of being right in both rising and declining stock markets, manages both the new IDEX fund family sponsored by Pioneer Western, and also the clones in the Western Reserve variable universal life insurance contracts.

M. D. Sass—a proven asset manager for giant pension and endowment accounts—is the portfolio steward for the newly formed Sass*Southmark group of funds. International Heritage, a brand-new Boston fund group, has venerable Vanguard as well as Endowment Management and London's Lombard-Odier as the actual fund managers.

INSURANCE CLONES & NEW IDEAS

When variable insurance products first appeared, they merely used shares issued by existing fund managements. For example, Sun Life used shares offered by Massachusetts Financial Services. These funds could be purchased from a broker for a personal account or IRA, or purchased as part of the variable insurance product funding.

In the late 1970s, the Securities & Exchange Commission moved to change the rules. The new regulations required that existing open-end mutual funds could not be used for funding variable contracts. Thus major fund sponsors also active in the insurance area "cloned" the existing funds. The new clones looked precisely like the traditional funds, but were set up and managed separately, and also given different names. In the case of the Sun Life investment choices, two established funds, MIT and MIG—the Massachusetts Investors Trust and Growth funds— became clones called CGS (Conservative Growth Series) and CAS (Capital Appreciation Series).

Many of the new variable insurance investment toys are managed not by their insurance company sponsors, but by third-party asset managers. Did the insurer make arrangements with a winner or a loser? Western Reserve Life, as noted earlier, employs Janus for this purpose (Figure 3–3). Sun Life uses the powerful and respected Massachusetts Financial Services as the source of insurance product clone management, as previously noted.

Quarterly-performance-history books on sale at the newsstands bark that message. Thus, when investigating these new variable life options to mutual funds, careful attention should be paid to the actual money manager. Life insurance companies have hardly proven to be top managers where blue chip and growth stocks are the issue. Notable exceptions are Phoenix

FIGURE 3–3
Janus Chart

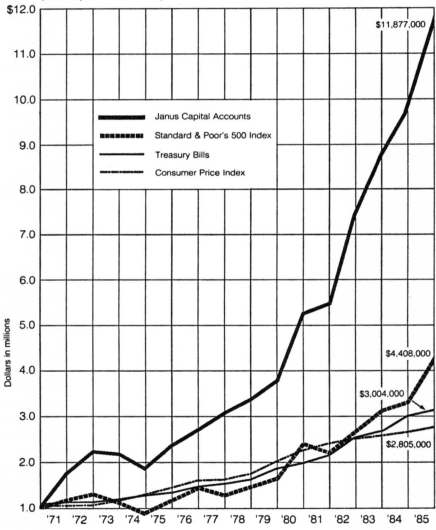

Assumed growth of one million dollars
(January 1, 1971 through December 31, 1985)

Legend:
- Janus Capital Accounts
- Standard & Poor's 500 Index
- Treasury Bills
- Consumer Price Index

$11,877,000

$4,408,000

$3,004,000

$2,805,000

Dollars in millions

'71 '72 '73 '74 '75 '76 '77 '78 '79 '80 '81 '82 '83 '84 '85

Source: Western Reserve Life Assurance Co. of Ohio.

Mutual, New England Mutual, and National Life of Vermont, whose funds have shown strong investment results.

And then there is the Rightime Fund—a black-box manager that does not even buy stocks and bonds, but buys shares in other mutual funds. The Rightime Fund purchases shares in a variety of funds based on the management results and investment outlook. The manager, assembling a portfolio of other fund managers, can use the computer to separate the winners from the losers, as you will learn when investment strategy and risk are discussed.

Also, today we are experiencing the era of the fund "clone." The clone takes shape in a variety of ways and for a number of business reasons:

- A fund can become too large to manage. "Too big" is "too bad" for stock funds in general, and particularly funds that express interest in growth or speculation. Fund managements set up another, separate fund with separate management and the same investment objectives and procedures. A clone is thus formed; for example, Pioneer II.
- Uncle Sam mandates that a mutual fund offered to the general public may not be offered as an option in the new breed of variable insurance company offerings. Thus a clone must be created, such as Janus and the IDEX funds, or Janus managing the equity portfolio for Western Reserve's variable universal life contracts.

The game, where portfolio managers are measured, becomes increasingly one of "who's on first?" Since fund sales growth is not lagging any index, the desire to be in the game often exceeds either the ability of the financial press to measure results, or the ability of the investing public to determine where first base is!

We might refer to the process at large as "clone craze" and "new fund craze." Any buzz-word triggers the marketing imagination of the sponsor. To sate the appetite of the investing public, the sponsors merely create new funds. New breeds, where funds or fund clones are concerned, are not necessarily good news for investors when considered in terms of "too big." "Clone craze" can indeed cause future shock for investors. The clone is not the original fund with a trusted and proven record. The manager of the clone is not necessarily the same person or team that built the fine record for the original issue. However, the clone often will be offered to investors as proxy for that original!

PART 2

DISCIPLINES, IDEAS AND STRATEGIES . . . AND THE NEW VARIABLE LIFE INSURANCE TOOL

CHAPTER 4

THE ALPHA-BETA GAME

"Don't gamble; take all your savings and buy some good stock and hold it till it goes up, then sell it. If it don't go up, don't buy it."

Will Rogers, 1924

PICKING WINNERS, AND HOW TO KNOW
WHEN YOU'RE WINNING

A tall order indeed. Are you doing fine when the stock market is up 100 percent in a few years, and you have increased your assets by one-third? Are you in the correct mutual fund if you are ahead a mere 80 percent during that period? Those questions lead to the alpha-beta game. Unfortunately, the folks who generated this wonderful investment tool—folks such as MIT, Harvard, Stanford, Chicago, The London School of Economics, and other prestigious institutions of academia—assumed that the American public understands both mathematics and statistics, and also Greek!

A good friend of the authors, Robert Dik, a successful property and casualty insurance producer in Worcester, Massachusetts, was asked about his success: "How did you reach for and achieve such high goals and standards?" Bob has acted as a university trustee and president of a variety of organizations on both the professional and private side of life, and has attained industry-wide status through both enormous volumes of business and professional designation.

"Well . . ." Bob replied, after an obligatory Yankee pause, "I play cards—bridge, for example—and I divide life the way the deck of cards is divided. You see, there are face cards, and there are number cards. My focus is always on the face cards!"

The alpha-beta game is the statistical, numeric, historic discipline that surfaces the "face cards" of mutual fund management, and relegates all others to "number-card" status. Is the fund manager a winner (a face card) or an also-ran? Is the fund manager a face card in the income or debt securities department, but a number card in equities and growth? The folks in academia used Greek terms, but Bob Dik translates the action to a deck of playing cards!

INVESTMENT SEMANTICS

First, you should learn two new words:

- ALPHA. What you earn or do not earn by taking a specific level of risk. Alpha is either plus or minus; i.e., you earn more than you are supposed to earn, or less than you deserve.
- BETA. The risks you take can be quantified over long time periods; i.e., all risk can be measured for all things in which you might invest. Risk, in this type of measurement, relates to either price volatility, or changes in the interest rates earned.

The classic example of beta is found in two classes of "investments" offered by the governments of our fair country. The first—the 90-day U.S. Treasury bill—is the standard of "zero risk," or beta 0.00. Uncle Sam, the printer of money, assures investors that their money will be repaid in 90 days with a stipulated rate of return—once 15 percent, now closer to 5 percent!

The beta number is zero for 90-day T-bills because the time is short, and therefore price changes are at a minimum. Think for a moment. When investors get nervous about almost anything, they move money toward cash-like instruments; or, if nervous about inflation or war, they shift to precious metals. The 90-day T-bill is a true "safe haven," while gold is very high on the list of beta options. When trouble is afoot, Mr. Dik would list 90-day T-bills as the choice for true safety.

Conversely, state governments sell lottery tickets where the chance of winning big is in the macro-millions. If you can accept the rate of return earned from T-bill ownership, you know in advance what the result will be. If you purchase a lottery ticket you will cash in a winning ticket (large odds), become the winner of the week (enormous odds), or tear your ticket into many pieces (most likely). The true odds, some say, are that the world as we know it will become littered with uncountable, torn-up losing tickets!

Thus, where T-bills represent "zero risk" the lottery tickets represent the ultimate risk possible. Penny stocks are close in risk terms; stock options and futures are also more than a bit risky; and new stock issues of untested companies come close. But there is a third element to the calculation of risk and its measurement that we need to understand.

STANDARD DEVIATION. At a given level of risk, what is the upside or downside potential; i.e., what might the investor make in better years, versus what might that same investor lose in poorer years?

Mr. Dik and his face cards notwithstanding, the substance for the alpha-beta game can be depicted with just three lines, as shown in Figure 4–1. We suggest that readers attempting to win the "total return" game learn the discipline of this illustration of risk and reward. After all, where money is on the line, knowing the risk and reward parameters is more important than the name of the stock or the fund, or what that company does, or in what shares that mutual fund invests its portfolio assets!

An old line, at least in sales, is that "you can't kid a kidder." We rather like the idea that Wall Street—and, in this case, academia—"doesn't want to confuse you (the investor) with the facts."

We have it on good authority that at least one of the graduate schools of business will grant a degree to any lay person who can either understand this simple illustration, or use it to better investment returns and reduce market risk.

Enough Fortune 1000 companies use the alpha-beta routine—as do most insurers, banks, and mutual funds—to constitute a majority. Yet all too few "typical investors" use it. A majority of professional investors perform this exercise daily,

FIGURE 4–1
Three Lines = The Facts MPT Illustration

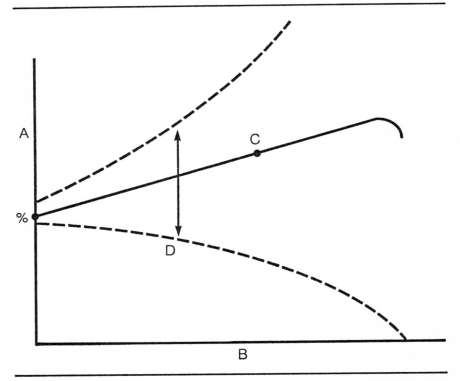

Source: Andersen & Walsh, Inc.

but the preponderance of individuals—those folks with quite a lot of their own money to lose—still view the process as Greek, or still believe that the great lottery ticket in the sky is going to descend and bring great winnings.

Figure 4–1 represents the engine-and-measurement mechanism of profit for those who intend to win the game of mutual fund family selection and continuing management. It is the absolute "ABC" of investment success.

We have divided the illustration into A (the alpha line), B (the beta, or risk, line), C (the capital-market line, or risk frontier that pinpoints risk exposure), and D.

- "A," for alpha, is simple stuff. Everyone would like to earn a large return, hopefully soon. Alpha is the return that is earned. It can be either plus or minus—good or not so good—when compared with "B."
- "B" stands for beta. On this axis the focus is on the status of a given investment—a mutual fund, for example—as it relates to the risk involved. Each bond, stock, or lottery ticket represents a specified degree of risk—zero for T-bill bonds, for example, and infinite or unmeasurable risk levels (beta) for some of the newly issued junk bonds. A beta above 1.00 represents a risk above the capital-market average; a beta below 1.00 represents below-average risk.
- "C," the capital-market line, or risk frontier, is a measurement line that allows us to place a specified investment—bond, stock, fund, or lottery ticket—in a measured spot on that line . . . much like finding your tax-bracket exposure in published tax tables before the 1986 reforms were enacted.

If you cannot stand a lot of risk, you might like a beta well below 1.00. If you need the highest possible return on investment, you are a high beta. Looking at the ABCs, and the typical investor invested in or contemplating a mutual fund purchase, we find five basic risk tolerances:

- "Mr. or Ms. Zero Risk." These folks will often opt for total-return performance well under the market norm (beta 1.00).
- "Mr. or Ms. Average." The game here, psychologically and interest-return oriented, is to do a bit better than price inflation allows, but to expose the assets to very little real risk. Beta, in this case, is usually in the .20–.35 range, which is 65 to 80 percent lower than normal market risk. These days, possibly 75 percent of all investors and savers fall into this convenient and comfortable risk category.
- "Normal Folks." The assumption is that the gross national product of America will grow. This idea places the "normal" investor on the market frontier at somewhere between .80 and 1.10 beta. Funds that are judged to be bal-

anced, income and growth, blue chip stock, or modestly into growth would be applied to this investor's risk-tolerance or need.

- "Growth is My Game." Growth or better returns, and proven growth with a sprinkling of speculation, means beta 1.20 + when the reader considers Figure 4–1. Here the investor is betting that the fund manager can find tomorrow's genetic-engineering stars, new technologies, underper-formers, or new service-industry concepts . . . or the "dry hole" that is suddenly "wet!" The bets, as with the Las Vegas analogy, get bigger as we move along the "C" line!
- The "Speculator." "Make one pile of all your money, and bet it on one toss of the dice." This reader is no longer a saver or investor; this is the true speculator. Some will likely win, at 2.00 + beta, but most folks will lose, and most of the losers will suffer badly!

"Suffering badly" brings us to "D" in the important illustration known now as Figure 4–1!

- Standard Deviation. The "Big D" does not stand for Dallas when discussing investment or savings choices. "D" stands for the critical issue when any investment is squarely on the table: win or lose, and by how much?

As the reader moves along the capital-market line to ever increasing beta risk, the reader also assumes far more price fluctuation. Price fluctuation and taxes are what risk is all about.

Standard Deviation—how much you might make versus how much you might lose when related to alpha and beta—is critical when canvassing the modern family of mutual funds, particularly if the reader is inspecting no-load offerings, or yearning for the new sector funds.

SAD BUT TRUE

The information packed into the three lines in Figure 4–1 represents the technology of investment. While most major money managers live with this information on a daily basis, we are underwhelmed by the number of brokers, planners, mutual fund salespeople, and mutual fund sales departments that are even aware of the logic of this technique.

Numerous investment-reporting and fee-based advisories, as well as mutual fund managements themselves, keep score of beta and alpha. Thus investors and others interested in using these important numbers to define risk and reward, or to determine which funds are hot and which are not, have numerous options. Those readers using a financial planner or broker for recommendations should insist on current beta and alpha readings.

If the game is do-it-yourself with no-load funds, the funds can often supply the needed data. The other course, should the fund refuse or play dumb, is to subscribe to a published advisory such as United Business Service or CDA Investment Technologies, to name two major and reliable sources.

The Rightime Fund, mentioned previously in the text, also calculates the alpha-beta numbers, as well as some unique additional statistics such as delta—a proprietary formula comparing a fund's relative improvement in total return. These are used by Rightime Econometrics, the fund manager, to select portfolio investments in other mutual funds. As such, the Rightime beta and alpha calculations represent the basic research effort.

While Rightime Econometrics does not publish these numbers for the public or shareholders, a quick look at the fund's quarterly report will display for the reader the current thinking on risk versus reward. Funds with below-average alpha will likely be sold, and funds with improving alpha (delta) will almost surely appear on the list owned. For those readers who wish to avoid the cost of expensive subscriptions, this may be a low-cost answer for growth and stock fund selection, both no-load and load.

THE IMPORTANCE OF ALPHA

Beta—the risk assumed—is important. Determining how much risk can be accepted is much like the annual physical. Each investor or saver is different in risk terms. However, since most of the saved assets in the system reside in low-beta investments, it is safe to assume that most of us are either risk avoiders (T-bills, passbooks, insurance values, money funds, short-term bank certificates, etc.) or normal risk takers (blue chip stocks and the mutual funds that buy them).

Where beta is like a "risk thermometer," alpha is what the fund buyer is most concerned with when selecting a money manager. Alpha, as noted earlier, can be either positive, neutral, or negative. That is, the manager is either earning more, less, or the same as indicated by the exposure to risk accepted by the portfolio owned. Why is alpha so important? Since all mutual funds charge the annual fees described in earlier chapters, and these are charged win or lose, the search for positive alpha is critical.

For example, in the illustration of Vanguard Funds in Figure 4–2 we find nine funds with negative alphas and ten with positive alphas. Considering the complex array of Vanguard offer-

FIGURE 4–2
Rightime Alpha/Beta Calculations for Vanguard Stock and Growth Funds

Fund		Alpha	Beta	Delta
van energy$	G	24.42	.70	−1.22
van explor2	G	−10.59	1.24	3.64
van explor x	G	−10.80	.99	3.39
van health$	G	8.07	1.02	.95
van index	G	1.37	1.07	−.76
van morgan	G	−5.06	1.23	.23
van naess	G	−15.98	1.30	.63
van primcap	G	2.44	1.21	−2.33
van qdpl x	G	9.14	.50	−2.56
van service$	G	−7.85	1.20	−.94
van star x	G	−5.06	.69	−1.37
van tcefusa	G	.21	1.01	−1.27
van tech$	G	−10.47	1.37	.95
van wellng x	G	.96	.80	−2.65
van wellsy x	G	2.40	.39	−6.78
van wind2	G	−1.73	1.00	−2.93
van windsr x	G	3.02	.80	−2.47
van wrldin x	G	33.25	.20	19.30
van wrldus	G	−7.56	.98	−.50

Source: Rightime Econometrics.

ings, the overall result is very good. However, it is especially good for those investors in the funds with positive alphas, and not nearly as good for the folks in the negative alpha funds. We remind readers that all nineteen funds are managed in the same store!

The investors in all funds are paying the management fee as due. The manager deserves the pay for the fine results recorded. The investors in the funds with downscale alphas are, in our view, being overcharged. Good to great performance is worthy of reward, while results that do not match or exceed risk exposure should be penalized . . . either by shareholders withdrawing funds, or by shareholders shifting to a new mutual fund earning better results.

In Figure 4–3 we can see classic alpha in action. IDEX II has a beta of 1.10—10 percent more risk than the Standard & Poor's 500—and a plus alpha of almost 5 percent. That is, the manager is presently earning at the 16 percent level versus the 11 percent that should be earned if a computer constructed a portfolio of stocks to match the 1.10 beta.

Conversely, CIGNA Growth—beta 1.14—has a negative alpha of more than 5 percent. That means the shareholder is presently underwater by that number. That is not to say the shareholder does not have a profit over cost. It really means that:

1. The profit earned is running well under the level that the beta (risk exposure) suggests;
2. That while a profit does or may exist depending on the date of purchase, the profit is much lower than it might be with better management;
3. That the IDEX holder, with roughly the same risk number, is earning 10 percent more overall than the CIGNA holder.

Why pay a management fee for less than good results? The alpha-beta game is designed to weed out weak or shoddy managements, and funds that have gotten out of tune with the market or key industry groups.

Learning about and monitoring funds on the basis of alpha and beta could be the most important lesson in this text. Requiring all advisors—in the case of no-load funds, the funds

FIGURE 4–3
IDEX/CIGNA MPT Illustration

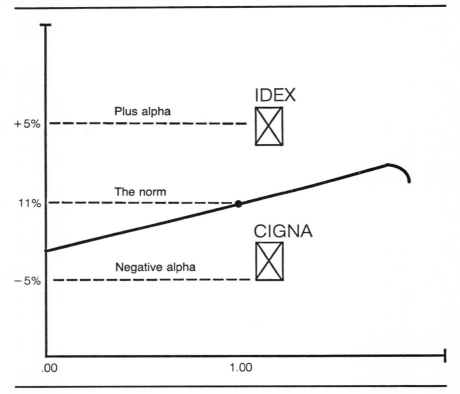

Source: Andersen & Walsh, Inc.

themselves—to report this information can sharply reduce the number of losing experiences, and make the happier results larger. Since the money is yours, insisting on the correct answers should be easy.

In earlier chapters we noted that the new Sass*Southmark funds offered a computer program to advisors called Beta*Calc. This program can be easily tied to the alpha-beta game because the basic data is built around the Figure 4.1 technology. Beta*Calc can quickly display your risk tolerance and spread assets along the capital-market line to show the ideal asset allocation. With that exercise behind you, the evaluation of funds based on beta

FIGURE 4–4
Beta: A Few Facts

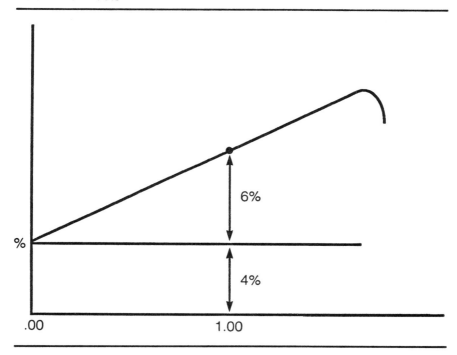

Source: Andersen & Walsh, Inc.

and alpha will display the best fund or funds to own, or which fund family to purchase.

Figure 4–4 sheds even more light on the alpha-beta game. We have added a new line across the chart from zero risk. As noted earlier, zero risk is equal to the return generated from the 90–day Treasury bill issued each week by Uncle Sam. A second new line has been inserted from normal market risk (Standard & Poor's 500 index) downward to zero return, and two generic numbers, 4 and 6, have been inserted. Since this is not a textbook, the authors have rounded these numbers for simplicity's sake.

- 4 percent. If you had invested in the riskless Treasury bills 50 years ago, and each time they matured reinvested the proceeds in new T-bills, you would have captured a gross return, pre-tax, of roughly 4 percent.

- 6 percent. If, instead of buying T-bills, you had accepted the normal risk associated with the S&P 500 on an unmanaged basis, you would have earned an additional 6 percent or so for that same time period.

Thus the market system, it appears, is willing to reward the normal risk taker with extra total return equal to roughly 6 percent. However, the story does not end with that higher return. First, the T-bill income is taxable at the federal level. Thus as much as half of that 4 percent riskless gross return would have been paid back to the Treasury by larger investors, and possibly 1 percent by the average or "typical" investor.

To further complicate things, there is inflation to consider. Portfolio managers and economy watchers believe that inflation roughly equals the T-bill rate over long time periods. If that assumption is correct, the risk avoider has earned zero by investing in riskless investments, and the normal risk taker has experienced a 6 percent pre-tax return. Since the portfolio representing the S&P 500 is unmanaged, or static, very few capital gains would have been realized to be taxed. Dividends on the S&P have been nearly the same as for T-bills over time. Thus most of the 6 percent spread would have been earned as a real return on investment by the normal risk taker (beta 1.00).

Using this insight, we can construct for each reader what we call a "risk thermometer" using our "Rule of 6." The "Rule of 6" is built around the theory that the 6 percent earnings spread above the risk-free rate is a constant—that the long-term holder of the index is entitled to that particular earnings premium.

THE RULE OF SIX IN ACTION

You have funds ready to be invested. How much risk exposure will be required to reach goals that have been established in advance? These might include building a retirement or education fund, or just good old "gettin' wealthy!"

- Step #1
  How much would you like to earn on the money? ____%

- Step #2
  Deduct the present return for T-bills (money market fund average yield could be used as a proxy here)   ____%
- Step #3
  That leaves a balance that can only be earned by accepting some additional market risk   ____%
- Step #4
  Divide the balance needed by 6 to get the beta needed to meet your objectives   Beta = ____

Equipped with that number, we now have the first clinical use of the alpha-beta tools. Return to Figure 4–4 and see where the calculated beta would place you on the line. Remember: if you fall above beta 1.00 you are going to assume more risk and a higher standard deviation than if you are below that normal level.

If the placement is way out to the right—say beta 1.50—the investment will be not only very, very risky, but you will find precious few funds to invest in. As we write, using Rightime Econometric beta calculations, there are only sixteen mutual funds with beta 1.50 or higher.

Thus if you are in the high beta range the issue is not so much arithmetic as reality. As we noted in Chapter 3, Keystone S-4 declined almost 70 percent in value during the crash of 1973–74. At that time the fund averaged a beta in the 1.45–1.60 range. A market downswing in a swinging fund with big beta exposure can be destructive to your money . . . and an awful psychological experience as well.

Usually when a very high beta is the result of the risk thermometer exercise, the problem relates to an unrealistic desire for growth. Keep in mind that the major market averages—the S&P 500 and Dow Jones Industrials—have averaged in the 10–11 percent area over long time periods. Shooting for a 20 percent average return means big, big beta. Big beta means big trouble when the market tricks you and goes south.

INDEX FUNDS

One way to play the alpha-beta game is to use a new type of fund in the modern fund family; a fund that indexes the portfolio to a point on the capital-market line. These funds, which are growing in popularity, avoid the alpha question by attempting to earn normal market results. Each of the Keystone Stock funds (S-1, S-3, S-4) is, for all practical purposes, squarely on the market line. The Vanguard Group is also active in the index-fund area.

The "Rule of 6" arithmetic is neither a permanent nor a one-time event. The calculation should be repeated at least once each year, and whenever there is a sharp increase or decrease in the T-bill rate. The reason for doing the numbers again is logical. When rates are rising, less risk can be taken. The converse is true when rates are in decline.

Assume that the overall investment goal is a return of 10 percent. Further, assume that the present T-bill return is 5.80 percent. The balance required by the rule would be a beta of .70 (4.20 percent divided by six). Thus the monies invested in one or more funds packaged to deliver that beta would be 30 percent less risky than the market itself. If T-bill yields dropped to 5.20 percent, the beta required would rise to .80; if yields rose to 6.40 percent, the beta needed would decline automatically to only .60.

The modern mutual fund family is made to order for the alpha-beta game and the "Rule of 6." All major families, as noted in Chapters 1 and 2, have cash funds (.00 beta), bond funds, stock funds, and growth funds. These funds typically charge only $5.00 to shift assets from one fund to another, and often there is no charge to shift into or out of the cash fund.

Thus a cradle-to-retirement investment program can be operated using the "Rule of 6" within one set of well-selected investment alternatives: the modern fund family, or as we will see, the variable insurance product with similar options.

BETA AND THE PHASES OF LIFE

Figure 4–5 divides life into three major periods experienced by any of us who achieve advanced age: learning, earning, and yearning; or need, greed, and fear. Each has a beta that can be assigned. Ted Weeks, our friend and fishing companion, has experienced all three of these periods.

FIGURE 4–5
The Beta Life Cycle

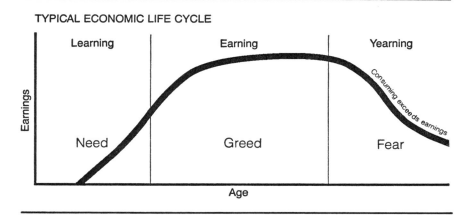

TYPICAL ECONOMIC LIFE CYCLE

Source: Fain Financial Services. Used with permission.

The learning, or need, period is just that. Unless Uncle Charlie or a favorite aunt has turned over a few bucks, the beta is typically going to be low, especially considering the rising cost of education. When the tuition bills arrive, or the graduate wants to start a business, the money should be there. A low beta will generally assure that result.

In the earning, or greed, period cash flow begins and risks can be accepted more readily. Small losses can be used on tax form 1040 for some benefit, and money can be replaced from future earnings. Thus the risk exposures during this longer life period can be far higher for most savers. Beta levels in the .80 to 1.20 range should be OK.

In the later yearning, or fear, years, money cannot easily be replaced because earnings from employment are either in fast decline or altogether gone. Thus, as retirement approaches or becomes a fact, beta should be lowered in most cases; the focus should shift to income and stability. Pre-retirement counsel should pay heed to both people and beta as that planning process comes into view!

THE TRUTH

Unfortunately, many of the brokers and advisors you deal with will not be disciples of the alpha-beta system. However, the authors have worked with this science for more than a decade and find it highly useful in terms of reducing market risk exposure and enhancing actual returns.

Returning to the life-cycle illustration in Figure 4–5, we have another dismal experience to report. People in the earning/greed group seem intent on waiting far too long to build real capital. They delay the decision to take some risk. With the very high interest returns offered in the late 1970s and early 1980s, they appear to be on the sidelines hoping for the stock market to decline (become cheap again!) and praying for interest rates to rise again to double-digit levels. Neither of these events is likely to happen soon. Our reasoning in regard to these key issues is reserved for Chapter 11.

Also, the yearning/fear group—those millions now facing or in retirement—appear to be accepting more risk than they can readily handle. On a pure beta basis these folks should be calming down. They seem, in sharp contrast, to be much too aggressive. They opt for unrealistically high current returns from junk bond funds on the assumption that a bond is a bond, interest will be paid on time, and principal will be returned at maturity. Recent experience tells quite another story!

These folks seem to be playing catch-up with their hard-earned money. Either inflation eroded purchasing power during the terrible years, or these were active players in the stock market that led to the horrific downturn in 1973–74. Otherwise, favoring passbook and similar accounts, they never took any risk at all, and now they are busily at work attempting to beat the market system . . . at age 60 and higher!

The life-cycle exercise tied to the "Rule of 6" is worthwhile and instructive wherever the reader fits in terms of age and circumstances. However, for those well along in their fifties, the arithmetic and timing exercises could be crucial if a happy retirement is a major concern.

SUMMING UP

The modern family of mutual funds tied to the alpha-beta game is clearly a winning combination. Readers using the logic found in Figure 4–1 can indeed earn higher total returns, reduce risk exposures, and be more comfortable with a long-range investment and savings plan.

While the logic works well with mutual funds, it works even better with the new breed of life insurance contracts known as variable life (VL), variable annuity (VA), and variable universal life (VUL), for obvious and often wonderful reasons: taxes are saved at least five ways. These tax benefits will be addressed in Chapters 7, 8, and 9. But we remind you here that these variable products presently are not taxable, while conventional mutual funds are, and heavily so under the new code.

To restate the basic truths in this chapter on risk and reward:

1. Every investment can be assigned a beta, and beta is the measurement used to describe risk.
2. All investments, including the most speculative, fall somewhere on the capital-market line. Other than purchasers of lottery tickets or junkets to Las Vegas, the vast bulk of savers and investors fall into the lowest beta measurements, or in the normal risk category around beta 1.00.
3. When paying a management fee, the key tactic is the search for positive alpha. Positive alpha is the amount earned when the management is great, and negative alpha comes with less lustrous management. But the fees charged are often the same.
4. Many publications today report beta, and all mutual funds have (or should have!) these calculations to report to existing and new shareholders. Also, dozens of advisories exist (your broker or planner should know them) that calculate beta, and often alpha, and which are available for a modest fee.
5. The alpha and beta numbers, tied to the "Rule of 6," can provide the saver and investor with a most useful and timely yardstick to relate to desired investment returns.

None of the above is etched in stone. It is not law, but logic and long-term experience combined. When combined with active asset-allocation models—such as the Sass*Southmark program discussed in Chapter 5 and earlier—the actual returns are not set in stone, but the strategy and risk exposure are . . . quite a neat idea when we look at the millions of investors earning substandard returns.

Books on the topic of alpha and beta—called capital-market theory, or modern portfolio technology, by Wall Street and academia—are hardly fun reading unless mathematics and statistics are your game. However, many texts are available. A call to your local college business school or stockbroker or advisor should uncover them. For those readers who have a computer at home, programming to calculate and record beta and alpha should be a simple task.

VARIABLE INSURANCE PRODUCTS

Even the new insurance products we mentioned must be tested on the basis of beta risk and alpha. While many are new, lacking experience and a track record, some beta history is probable for some, and those using proven asset managers for their fund clones will have solid beta information.

For these insurance products the alpha-beta game may even be more important than for conventional mutual fund families. The taxable mutual fund contains no insurance element. Thus the shareholder can quit any afternoon at 4:30, when the fund sets the net asset value to determine purchase and sale pricing.

In these new insurance products, where considerable tax deferral for dividend and interest income exists under present law, the decision to quit is exacerbated by tax questions. Thus inadequate management may be kept to avoid the pain and suffering of liquidation of investment units, or for lack of knowledge concerning transfer to other funds. The same logic also would apply to other tax-preferred mutual fund investments such as the IRA, tax-sheltered annuity, Keogh plan, or 401(k) plan as applied to insurance contracts. These programs are easy to buy. Changing them from one fund sponsor to another can be arduous at best, particularly where no-load funds are used.

But keep in mind that the alpha-beta game is utilized regularly at virtually all major financial institutions. Uncle Sam uses the technique to measure the prudence of those who manage retirement plan assets. College trustees employ it to gauge risk exposure for the endowment fund and keep abreast of those all-important returns. And, almost certainly, every mutual fund manager—including those who approach stock and bond investments from the classic fundamental research mode—use the process to make certain they are in gear and not running their assets off the highway and into a ditch.

As we move toward the ever-present and changing world of taxes, we are reminded that we know quite a lot more about mutual funds and the underpinnings of today's huge, growing, and diverse fund families.

By now we have a better sense of what funds are, what the costs of ownership are, what asset allocation is, and how to look at past performance. And through the alpha-beta game, we know how to look at ourselves and our money, and possibly gaze with insight into the future.

One last step lies just ahead. The stock market rises and falls. Were it possible to gaze into the future to judge market trends, and to tie that vision into alpha, beta, asset allocation, and the finest fund management, the game indeed would be won. Bob Dik, our face-card commentator, might remark that "high alpha" is the face card of investment, and when that can be combined with "modest beta," the game is clearly won! Editor Weeks would add that alpha is the correct fly to employ to attract *Salmo salar;* beta the perfect water to cast that fly into.

CHAPTER 5

WIN, LOSE, OR DRAW: . . .
ACTIVE ASSET ALLOCATION
. . . OR OTHER WORDS!

"Many people called him a wizard of finance—which is not the same thing as a wizard of magic, though sometimes fairly similar."

Dodie Smith

While the idea now known as "comprehensive financial planning" was spawned in the 70 percent tax-bracket years of the late 1960s and mid-1970s, a "new" power selling phrase has hit the media and investment-advisory community lately: active asset allocation.

"What goes around, comes around!" as some elder observers note with some degree of praise for forward thinking. Asset allocation devised to reduce risk and enhance reward is simply another way of saying "professional management with clearly delineated risk tolerance"; or, better, "professional management with guidelines."

Think of the market for stocks and bonds as a river. In spring that river is in spate. In the heat of summer the flow dribbles to minor rivulets. As the thunderclouds pour down their loads of moisture, the river again swells. In winter the river is covered with ice and snow and appears to be still. Yet the river never ceases to flow!

Such is the market of stocks and bonds, interest rates due and payable on interest-bearing securities, and the promises of profit offered in one sector of the markets or another. The flow in one is rising, and in another declining.

The salmon of both coasts and the steelhead in the Pacific Northwest are, in our analogy, investors and asset allocators. These great game fish move through the rivers under all possible conditions in search of a goal (investor profit). These phenomena—market conditions, interest rates, potential profits—allocate the water that the salmon must traverse to perform the ever-uphill climb required to find a spawning place . . . and do so with all of the impediments that banks, insurers, Wall Street, and advisors bring to the table of gain or loss—bad advice, poor reference to the client's risk tolerance, lack of savvy about "conditions ahead," and so on.

It is indeed amazing that some salmon survive, reach preset goals, spawn, and create future generations that also survive. To perform this minor miracle, these spotted wonders have traversed the sea and the river under all and any conditions, and bested a host of predators from seal and otter to eagle and raven.

The analogy to asset allocation should not be lost. In Chapter 4, the concept and technology called "capital-market theory" was addressed. In Chapter 6, we will deal with market timing which, like it or not, is a form of asset allocation. As we move through this chapter we will face up to the "D" series of strategies, which by any definition are progressive asset allocation devices.

The modern family of mutual funds, and the insurer offerings that mirror them, are asset allocation models. Rarely used as such, and almost never offered in the active allocation mode, the modern family is truly an investment marvel.

- Chapter 4. The market line and "Rule of 6"—the modern fund family incorporates every major reference point on that line!
- Chapter 6. To come. The mutual fund, for this esoteric allocation game, is the only game in town for the typical investor and average quality retirement plan.

WHAT CONSTITUTES ASSET ALLOCATION?

Asset allocation is a major headache for almost all investors. The idea of placing some assets here and others there, all hopefully working together, is overwhelming to many. Novice investors carry around a bunch of shop-worn platitudes that further confuse their allocation decisions:

- Dear Old Dad said, "You can't lose in real estate;" therefore, all of my savings are poised in that direction.
- Rich Uncle Charles once said, "People will always drink beer, so you should own shares of Bud."
- Some say "Diamonds are forever." This conveniently forgets that people and goals are not.

The system designed for savings and investment, and the system which transfers knowledge and expertise from generation to generation and culture to culture never have bothered to deal with the asset allocation issue. Poor or misguided asset allocation can lead to actual poverty. Many long-term savers have not adjusted their asset allocation stance since the upheavals of the 1930s!

There are several great Texas families on the rocks these days. The Hunts come to mind, as do the Murchisons, and the Bass brothers. These folks bet the farm and allocated assets on oil and other natural resources. These smart folks bet the whole bundle, a la Kipling's "one toss," on just one pony, and they lost.

Too much savings in a bull market for stocks is bad news. Too much speculation in any specific area of the domestic or world economy at any time is likely to be the wrong strategy where money and its accumulation are a concern. Asset allocation insists there is no perfect answer—that as market circumstances change, assets must be reallocated to cover or hedge against that change; as age and family circumstances are altered, similar changes in asset allocation must be made. There are no easy, pat answers. Our Texas billionaires discovered this fact when they overplayed silver, oil, and other hard asset investments.

PROFESSIONAL INVESTORS—BE ONE!

Picture yourself as the manager of your college endowment fund, or the treasurer of a major corporation, or the decision-maker on the investment committee for a large retirement program.

The "all oil/all savings/all anywhere" format simply does not play. Yet thousands of prudent men in trustee-type positions "cop out" and make investment decisions because they do not know how to cope with the asset allocation question.

What the college or pension trustees (usually) understand—considering the specific relationship of risk to reward—is that to earn a high total return in the long term, assets must be distributed intelligently among good-news and bad-news investment segments. It makes a lot of sense to divide investments and investors by sentiment:

- "Go with the flow." This investor buys or does what all other savers and investors do. The investible funds are likely to be found underearning in a bank, thrift, or insurance company.
- "Rise with the tide." This investor, when it seems timely, goes with the flow of speculation hoping that enough momentum exists in the play (the system) to produce a profit from the flow itself.
- "Mr. & Ms. Bailout." Whatever worked last year will work again this year. "How can I go wrong with something that went up 50 percent last year?"

Asset allocation, in the context of this chapter, does not relate directly to the mutual fund term "diversification." Diversification means the spread of assets among many companies or a number of industries. Thus, in terms of asset allocation, a sector fund is not diversified, but concentrated.

Asset allocation is something quite different. Some assets, given a set of fiscal or age circumstances, should be in cash. Other assets should be seeking income and safety. Still others could or should be invested for growth and, if you know the right horse, possibly a small amount should be allocated toward a market sector that has special short- or long-term appeal—energy or technology, for example.

Investor lemmings in past booms have learned the hard way, and each of these "sentimental investors" has suffered in monetary terms. The asset allocators have a better idea. Their idea works because the allocation process dictates diversification of assets among a variety of risk pools and investment choices that suit the ever-changing needs of real investors.

ON THE MARKET LINE

Chapter 4 is worth reviewing now. On that "efficient frontier of risk" we have all known investment experience, and all of the options—some risky, some riskless. Most folks, unfortunately, pick one and forget all the others.

On the market line there are no correct answers to the investment riddle. What each reader faces is a series of choices, some simple and some requiring profound thought. In asset allocation terms each family is different. Yet banks, thrifts, life insurers, mutual funds, and stock brokers try to squeeze the entire population into neat categories. We agree that every family should save some money. We also agree that all parties need some protection. Both of these are key elements in the asset allocation process. The market line, on review, clearly illustrates that there are other options, and that some of these—the search for growth and higher total return from quality equity investments such as mutual funds—are critical to investment success.

Most people are, by nature, risk avoiders. If you own auto insurance, you're one of them. The people who manage large piles of money avoid risk by spreading the money around.

In the basic mutual fund family, the spreading of risk is called diversification and is required under the terms of the various Investment Companies Acts. Diversification is good, says Congress, because that alone spreads risk among many companies, or among many industries in a broadly diversified mutual fund.

Whereas major entities of investment allocate assets on a daily, hourly, and momentary basis, the typical company or family investor is involved in making arduous, one-at-a-time decisions. "Savings accounts are wonderful," their thinking often goes, "even when they underperform every bond index or the yield for money market funds." And so forth. Asset allocation is one of the secrets to investment success, which can be defined as total investment and savings return relative to inflation and the stock market. Why?

- Some assets, if diversified and allocated along the market line, will be in the right place.
- In concert, assets allocated along the market line will produce a higher total return than if all assets are in the wrong place.

Think of the millions of American families and retirement plans that were 100 percent focused on passbook savings, money market funds, and short-term bank certificates when interest rates were cut in half by actions of the Federal Reserve to contain inflation. With appropriate asset allocation, many of these investors would have doubled their investment returns. With no funds allocated to blue chip or growth stocks, an equal number of Americans missed the best bull market in history.

THE PROBLEM . . . AND A SOLUTION

In the beginning there is advice from family and friends, and vibrations from the system itself. Savings accounts are wonderful (sometimes). Stocks are intrepid saviors of profit (at other times). And, everybody knows that bonds are safe, secure, and produce high levels of income (some are, some are not, sometimes they work, and at other times they clearly fail). The game is, as always, total return. Asset allocation—executed by using the capital-market line, the four classes of risk above, and the computer—can produce the correct mixture of assets to yield that elusive total-return answer.

If asset allocation is good for the "big guys," why not for everyone? And, wisdom notwithstanding, the modern tool of investment thought is the home computer. Asset allocation thereon is now a practical rather than theoretical matter.

Recently, a useful PC diskette crossed these writers' paths. For the average family, building college or retirement funds, or funds for other purposes, "Beta*Calc"—software offered through a new family of mutual funds known as the "Hidden Strength" funds—handles the asset allocation equation quite easily. The market line deals essentially with four classes of risk.

- Money market funds—a proxy for Treasury bills of short duration—with minimal risk.
- Quality bonds—not junk, leveraged, discounted, hedged, or otherwise defamed or diminished—that can pay off when the bonds mature.
- A balanced portfolio of stocks and bonds of quality—companies that can pay off the debt and under all usual circumstances make a profit and pay dividends to shareholders. No pie in the sky with these folks!
- Blue chips and high-quality growth stock in the kinds of companies that can buy four-page multi-colored centerfolds, and multiple Superbowl slots.

Those four categories represent the basic options for at least 95 percent of all retirement plans and a similar percentage of families. In those choices we find clear resolution of essentially all needs, psychological or economic, for all goal-based scenarios. Figures 5–1 and 5–2 illustrate state-of-the-art asset allocation printouts available from brokers and planners.

THE COMPUTER IN FINANCIAL PLANNING

Often, when comprehensive financial planning was the hot buzzword, the computer ended up being the scapegoat. Folks actually believed the computer was thinking for them . . . providing solutions, that almost no human could contemplate for their specific or common problems. Hogwash! Humbug!

A major life and casualty insurer (think red and raining) tried artificial intelligence for financial and investment decision-making. During 1987 the directors folded the company and sustained a large loss for investors and themselves. Active asset allocation using Beta*Calc is different for the modern, thoughtful investor. You can see in the different scenarios in Figure 5–2:

- The computer deals only with facts.
- Will the market rise or fall, or will interest rates go up or down; by how much?

FIGURE 5.1
Beta*Calc Before

To begin with:	How Would You Like Your Money Invested?
Category	Investment Potential:

CONSERVATIVE:	Return : MODEST Upside : MODEST (+5 to 10%) Downside : MINIMAL (0%)
MODERATE:	Return : Better than average Upside : +10 to + 20% in a good market Downside : −10% in a poor market
AGRESSIVE:	Return : Superior Upside : +20% to +30% in a good market Downside : −15% in a poor market

You are investing:		
	40,000	80.00% CONSERVATIVE
	10,000	20.00% MODERATE
	0	.00% AGGRESSIVE
for a TOTAL of:	50,000	Dollars

Source: Sass•Southmark Mutual Funds

FIGURE 5–2
Beta*Calc After One Million or More Calculations

ALLOCATION: Based on the answers you provided, BETA*CALC has computed the following allocation recommendation:

	Dollars	Percent
Growth Portfolio	14,421	28.84
Quality Income Portfolio	31,397	62.79
Money Market Portfolio	4,182	8.36

PERFORMANCE: The anticipated change in the value of the recommended allocation, based on your chosen scenario.

	Change in Portfolio Value	
Scenario	Dollars	Percent
Worst Case	−1,000	−2.00
Expected	4,897	9.79
Best Case	7,947	15.89

Source: Sass*Southmark Mutual Funds

- How much risk can be accepted in the undulating exposure to interest rate and market risks?
- What are the real goals, needs, essentials, and how much capital accumulation is required to reach that goal?
- How much more if you wait just one year?

What was once possible only on a large main-frame computer is now at the intelligent investor's fingertips: 1,000,001 calculations, performed in seconds, that document the lowest possible risk exposure among the four investment segments listed on page 87, to realize the perceived, desired, or referenced investment goal!

Can any reader still feel confident that a single decision device can provide the correct single-decision answer? Not a chance! The discussion of the capital-market line in Chapter 4 deals with the key issues at a level of confidence that overwhelms the sanctity of either savings-oriented or speculative bastions of thought.

"If you live by the passbook, surely you will die—possibly in poverty—by the same device."

ATTITUDINAL ALTERATION AND ARTICULATION

The stuff of asset allocation is bred in our birthright and today's technology. Beta*Calc, one of many new tools in this area, merely illustrates a logical methodology that answers the questions which father and son, uncle and brother, sister and niece have dealt with for centuries: "What do I do with my money?" For most readers we add the caveat, "What do you do when you get some money?"

Active or passive asset allocation is both strategy and game. Take the massive capability of Beta*Calc, for example. The saver or investor can play the computer once, formulate a plan, and relate the plan to a goal. Or, better, the investor can do the exercise at regular intervals that mesh with changes in the economy, both domestic and global.

Thus allocation of assets is simple (think Beta*Calc) yet more complex. To the four basic risk options, today's investor must add global investments, hedging tools, precious metals, real estate options, energy, and ever-changing tax considerations.

A PANOPLY OF STRATEGIES FOR PROFIT

The asset base of the huge mutual fund industry was built around two quite simplistic investment strategies. These, we suspect, still account for the bulk of shareholder accounts and the vast majority of accumulated assets:

- Buy and hold quality stock, and growth, balanced, or income funds, usually reinvesting dividend and capital gains distributions in shares of the fund originally bought.
- Dollar-cost-averaging: the systematic investment of equal dollar amounts on a monthly or quarterly basis.

Buy-and-hold relates to lump sums, usually shifting from individual stock and bond holdings or bank savings instruments. Dollar-averaging typically relates to a goal-oriented program, such as accumulating wealth for education or retirement, and is often started in conjunction with a life insurance program.

While both approaches are widely marketed in the media by no-load funds, and with sales charges by financial planners, stockbrokers, and (increasingly) thrift institutions, these two "dumb" approaches to fund investment have delivered quite different results.

Despite all logic, the preponderance of buy-and-hold money flows into stock and growth funds at or near market tops. Much of that sum abruptly exits the fund at or near the subsequent market bottom! Summarily, an unhappy set of investors come to mistrust mutual funds as losses for tax purposes are recorded. Bernard Baruch's famous "buy low, sell high" seems conveniently forgotten by these unhappy investors and their advisors.

Certainly there are hordes of ably counseled investors who have turned small sums into much larger amounts on a buy-and-hold basis. However, monthly and annual sales statistics compiled and reported in the media, or by the Investment Company Institute, continue to record that the investor has a distinct propensity to engage in mutual fund purchases backwards.

Consider the stock market of the moment. The market as measured by the Dow Jones, Standard & Poor's, or other indices, more than doubled in the 1984–86 period. Yet advisors were selling and the investing public was buying bond and fixed income funds with abandon. At the same time, investors were for the most part shunning stock and growth funds. The sales ratio (bond funds to stock funds) was a fairly constant four to one during much of the period of huge market rise!

The disciplined dollar-averager, by contrast, has done very well indeed. For this type of investor—invariably buying a growth, stock, or speculative fund—it matters little if the market is too high or near its lows. In reality, if the stock market declines in the early years, the end result is likely to be better, as more shares are purchased by the level contribution when stocks (and therefore the fund) are cheap.

Dollar-averagers who have faithfully made their periodic investments for 10, 15 and 20 years or longer have indeed recorded large and often spectacular gains. The illustration of the dollar-averaging process in Figure 5–3 is hardly the finest result the fund industry can demonstrate, but rather is mid-range among funds active in the dollar-cost-averaging market.

While most of the fund industry assets have been put in place by one or the other of these simple routines, there are less widely used techniques that can augur well for investors in terms of safety, comfort level, and total-investment return.

Market timing, discussed in Chapter 6, has proven productive for those who use it in a disciplined fashion; that is, those who do not attempt to second-guess the signals. However, the volume of fund assets subject to timing probably does not exceed $5 billion, a mere shadow of the volume of moneys subject to buy-and-hold investment plans.

SENSIBLE LONG-TERM
ALLOCATION STRATEGIES

With the advent of sector or "niche" funds, investment techniques to deal with these often highly price-volatile vehicles are critical. Also, there are far greater numbers of very speculative

FIGURE 5–3
Illustrate DCA

	Cost of Shares					Value of Shares					
Date	Cum. Net Investment	Annual Income Divids	Cum. Income Divids	Total Investment Cost	Annual Cap. Gain Distrib	From Invest.	From Cap. Gain Reinvest.	Sub-total	From Divids Reinvest.	Total Value	12% Interest Projection
12/31/56	2000	67	67	2067	45	1934	45	1979	64	2043	2240
12/31/57	4000	133	200	4200	90	3237	126	3363	170	3533	4749
12/31/58	6000	215	414	6414	154	6802	328	7130	471	7601	7559
12/31/59	8000	280	695	8695	212	9393	573	9966	800	10765	10706
12/31/60	10000	359	1054	11054	290	10870	856	11726	1135	12861	14230
12/31/61	12000	450	1503	13503	837	14803	1814	16617	1763	18380	18178
12/31/62	14000	573	2076	16076	805	14367	2381	16748	2081	18829	22599
12/31/63	16000	727	2803	18803	807	17415	3371	20786	2915	23701	27551
12/31/64	18000	809	3612	21612	1184	20628	4798	25426	3935	29360	33097
12/31/65	20000	924	4535	24535	1608	26210	7247	33457	5569	39027	39309
12/31/66	22000	1074	5609	27609	2167	24560	8561	33121	5878	38999	46266
12/31/67	24000	1268	6877	30877	2266	34067	13404	47471	8890	56361	54058
12/31/68	26000	1628	8506	34506	3642	43145	19696	62841	12301	75142	62785
12/31/69	28000	1822	10328	38328	3178	35316	18291	53607	11331	64938	72559
12/31/70	30000	2216	12544	42544	4322	33966	20902	54868	12626	67493	83507
12/31/71	32000	2433	14977	46977	1681	38578	24170	62747	15943	78691	95767
12/31/72	34000	2737	17714	51714	3563	43494	29641	73135	19794	92929	109499
12/31/73	36000	3020	20734	56734	4418	40433	30712	71145	20560	91706	124879
12/31/74	38000	3442	24176	62176	4734	31453	26402	57854	18234	76088	142105
12/31/75	40000	4143	28319	68319	1465	43818	36443	80262	28082	108344	161397
12/31/76	42000	4656	32976	74976	2168	59403	49886	109289	41601	150890	183005
12/31/77	44000	5575	38550	82550	4733	59348	53088	112436	45972	158408	207206
12/31/78	46000	6429	44979	90979	5474	63893	61526	125420	54690	180110	234310
12/31/79	48000	7747	52726	100726	5960	78530	80367	158897	73891	232788	264668
12/31/80	50000	9937	62663	112663	8321	97896	107581	205477	101248	306725	298668
12/31/81	52000	12991	75654	127654	9138	89243	104978	194221	103145	297367	336748
12/31/82	54000	14563	90217	144217	18570	92439	128231	220670	121341	342011	379398
12/31/83	56000	15022	105238	161238	17305	108098	166509	274606	154749	429355	427166
12/31/84	58000	16420	121659	179659	19437	100089	169871	269959	157662	427621	480665
12/31/85	60000	17832	139491	199491	22249	117549	222037	339586	201821	541406	540585
Cumulative Totals			$139,491		$150,823						

Source: Western Reserve Life Assurance Co. of Ohio.

growth funds now than there were a decade earlier. These two types of mutuals can make investors quite unhappy (and a lot poorer) if purchased at cyclical tops in the case of a sector fund, or at major market tops for the high-beta growth fund. For example, Keystone's S-4 fund—speculative by definition, and managed in the 1.50–1.60 beta range—declined 70 percent in the great bear market of 1973–74! Thus the hardy buy-and-hold investor who bought that fund at the previous market top needed a *tripling* in the net-asset value merely to get even!

TWO-DIMENSIONAL INVESTING

One of our favorite strategies for the long-term goal oriented investor is "2-D," the two-dimensional approach. "2-D" combines the virtues of both of the conventional fund-purchase strategies widely marketed. It is simple enough to understand, but smart, as you will see from the numbers illustrated in Figure 5–4.

The virtues of the "2-D" approach are clear from the numbers. The investor lived through the 1973–74 crash, the account was never in trouble, and the equity half of the account accumulated large numbers of growth fund shares that added significant value in the subsequent bull market. Here is how the strategy works:

- The lump sum to be invested is divided and 90 percent of the asset is positioned in a low-risk quality bond fund. The remaining 10 percent is invested in a growth or sector fund with long-term appeal.
- The income generated from the bond fund, usually paid monthly these days, flows to the equity fund selected.
- Thus the bond fund is the buy-and-hold portion of the package, and the dividend flow is the dollar-cost-averaging piece obtaining growth.

The strategy is obviously a low-risk, high-return approach to fund investment. The bulk of the original investment is in low-risk bonds that are managed to produce a steady flow of income. Thus the major initial asset in the package has a high investor comfort level, and only a small part of the original sum,

FIGURE 5–4

Illustration of a 19-Year Two-Dimensional Account (A $10,000 investment in a bond fund with dividends reinvested in a stock fund)

Year	Dividends Paid	Bond Account Value	Stock Account Value	Combined Account Value
1968	$616	$ 9,903	$ 586	$10,489
1969	650	8,596	1,069	9,665
1970	664	7,725	1,737	9,462
1971	673	8,660	2,848	11,508
1972	711	8,950	3,896	12,846
1973	702	7,613	3,463	11,076
1974	741	6,285	2,920	9,205
1975	751	7,062	4,998	12,060
1976	701	8,190	6,881	15,071
1977	701	8,081	7,502	15,583
1978	711	7,739	8,987	16,726
1979	769	7,133	12,547	19,680
1980	817	6,898	17,225	24,123
1981	895	6,672	17,510	23,822
1982	895	7,737	22,979	30,716
1983	895	8,903	30,725	39,628
1984	895	9,105	30,425	39,530
1985	895	10,926	49,122	60,048
1986	895	12,204	53,701	65,905
3-31-87	149	12,570	64,739	77,309

Source: Andersen & Walsh, Inc.

plus the dividend flows, are exposed to real market risk; but in a systematic way that historically has worked very, very well.

In addition to comfort and a feeling of safety, the investor in a "2-D" format solves the problem that often discredits dollar-cost-averaging, which is the discipline required to make the monthly or quarterly account investments. The adage often used in financial planning and mutual fund circles is, "People don't plan to fail, they just fail to plan!"

Since dividend production from the bond fund is a scheduled event, either monthly or quarterly, and the money flows not across your desk or kitchen table, but directly to the stock, growth or sector fund, none of that steely discipline is required; everything works with the precision of a computer. We find that when a dividend check gets to our kitchen table, it usually spends well at the country club for dinner . . . not to buy more shares in a fund that might also compound to a larger value over time!

If there is a drawback to "2-D" it's the patience that's required. Some say "it's just no fun at all." It is indeed getting-rich-slow. However, for the clear majority of savers and investors, it is a comfortable scenario now and a profit wunderkind down the road.

REVERSE "2-D"

This approach is clearly riskier in the early years than its sister "2-D." Where "2-D" fits a younger audience (25–45) to give the dollar-cost-averaging aspect lots of time to work, "D-2"—reverse two-dimensional—probably fits the age 40–55 audience best. As described, the shape of the dimensions is reversed.

- Ninety percent of the original investment is positioned in a quality common stock fund; a blue chip fund with a beta range of .90 to 1.10.
- The remaining 10 percent buys a high-quality corporate bond fund, municipal bond fund if taxes are a critical issue, or other income-producing vehicle that has low risk exposure.
- The dividends and realized gains generated from the stock fund automatically flow into the bond or income vehicle.

Thus, as each passing year brings retirement closer, the percentage of assets in quality stocks relative to the total account value is shrinking, while the percentage in income-producing bonds is rising.

When retirement becomes reality, the overall risk exposure will have been significantly reduced, and the level of spendable income will have been sharply improved at precisely the time it is needed!

The age cutoff for this strategy is, in our opinion, about ten years prior to projected or expected retirement. The reason is that owning a stock fund, even of the blue chip variety, requires time. Time is also required to make the asset-shifting work its reputed wonders. Ten years represents, typically, two full market cycles: top, bottom, top, or the reverse. Two full cycles should virtually assure success to the saver or investor using either "2-D" or "D-2."

AND NOW, HOW ABOUT "3-D"!

Unlike "2-D" and "D-2," we are not certain that any live investor has ever actually put a "three-dimensional" account in operation. However, where sensible long-term asset allocation strategies using funds become conversation, "3-D" is often discussed. The underpinning of sheer logic is powerful indeed:

1. First, set up a "2-D" account as described—90 percent + in a bond fund, and the balance in a stock, growth or sector fund.
2. The dividends from the bond fund flow to the equity vehicle automatically. Now, we add the third leg to the strategy.
3. The equity fund will, from time to time (several times a year in bull markets), distribute realized capital gains. These gains are usually reinvested in the fund that generated them. In the "3-D" approach these gains would be paid over to the bond component of the program.

Where is the logic in this tactic? Growth and stock funds often realize and distribute large gains during a bull market, or around a major market top. Why reinvest these gains in the plan element that is likely to perform poorly in a subsequent bear market? Why not, instead, direct the winnings (the capital gains are, for all intents, winnings!) to the low-risk, income-producing part of the package.

In doing so, risk exposure is reduced at or near major market tops. The income of the "cash-cow" (a business or investment that generates huge cash flow from minimum effort), low-risk element is instantly improved as well. Thus, the dollar-cost-averaging engine gets more fuel to make that element work harder during any subsequent declining period.

These "D" strategies are lower-risk by definition than Kipling's "make a pile of your assets" strategy, vis-à-vis either the dice table or the stock market. They are slow, plodding, unexciting. However, they seem to produce winning results over time—far greater total returns than the random asset allocation approach used by most mutual fund investors and many planners and professional advisors.

REBALANCING

Another strategy for fund investment that has been with us for decades, but is rarely used in practice, is the annual act of rebalancing the account; or to put it another way, balancing the risk and reward scales.

- The mutual fund account is opened with the purchase of a quality bond fund for one-half the amount available, and a stock, growth, or sector fund for the other half.
- Once each year—usually December 31 or the first business day in January—the account is rebalanced to the original 50/50 asset allocation.

The logic in rebalancing is that stocks will either rise or decline each year. If they have risen, the stock fund share will be worth more than 50 percent, and the risk of stocks declining in the coming year has also risen.

Thus excess equity is shifted to the low-risk bond fund. Conversely, if the stock market has declined in the now-concluded year, the statistical prospect for a market rise has become larger. In this case, assets are shifted from the bond bucket to the equity bucket.

Again, like the "D" series of techniques, rebalancing is dull to worse, with only one investment decision a year, and only two multiplication exercises and one division tabulation involved in that decision.

The great advantage of each of these disciplined approaches to fund investment is economic, in two distinct ways. First, the investor will have more money at the end than at the beginning. Second, in rebalancing you need buy only one Wall Street Journal a year, and in the "D" series none at all. The savings will mount to a tidy sum over time!

ENTER SECTOR FUNDS

A sector or "niche" fund, by definition, concentrates fund assets in a certain industry, specific geographical area, or highly compatible business group ("health sciences" can include a variety of businesses, but all must be health-related). Asset allocation for these funds is narrowed to a sliver!

However, these sector funds have experienced fantastic growth in two ways in recent years. First, the number of sector offerings has exploded in both number and category, and the media advertising promoting these has grown, as Duke Ellington might opine, "beyond category."

Sector funds are likely to work with the identical strategies explained above. However, there are some caveats that the investor should consider:

1. Is the sector under consideration cyclical or long-term in terms of secular growth?

Is the sector, like springtime, a place of future greening of income and asset growth, or is it an area that runs hot and cold? Precious-metal-sector funds are cyclical, for example. War, international panic, and high inflation rates in hard-currency countries are fodder for these funds, which rise in price when everything looks terrible, and fall when better economic and political events appear.

2. Market sectors will be in or out of favor, often underperforming for long periods after a year or two of major price advance.

Sector investments are probably more appropriately termed "market" or "economic segment" investments. They are subject to the annual popularity or stock-market beauty contest. These funds can experience huge upward price swings when in favor, and reverse price action when Wall Street and investors neglect them. Since sector funds are relatively new, an illustration of the market placement of a precious-metals fund will serve our purposes nicely.

Ranking Among All Funds

Fund	Year					
	1979	1980	1981	1982	1983	1984
Strategic Investments	#1	#8	#469	#5	#562	#641

There were fewer than 800 mutual funds in this time period versus the 2,100-plus in registration today . . . and possibly 3,000-plus by the time this book is read. The fund was a hero in three of the six years in question, and a true dog in the remaining three. It is fair to assume that the bulk of investment moneys entered the fund early in years 1980, 1981, and 1983. Terrible relative performance followed. The commodity, in this instance, was out of favor with investors, but fund buyers attracted by previous results of this sector were unaware . . . until tax losses were registered!

Thus sectors are tricky, lending themselves more to market timing—attempting to predict hot sectors from cold—or to the "2-D" approach where the sector in question represents a strong secular growth area (computers, high-tech, health care, financial services, etc.).

THE CONTRARIAN SECTOR PLAYER

Looking at our yearly performance example earlier, we might conclude that sector funds lend themselves brilliantly to a contrarian view of the world. We refer to the phenomenon as the Isaac Newton-Newton Isaac market reality. "What is up will come down, and what is down will rebound," is the heart of this method.

- Purchase equal amounts of three sector funds that have performed poorly in the previous year.
- At the conclusion of the first year, sell the best performer, and use the proceeds to purchase the niche with the worst results.
- Repeat the money-making remedy above in each successive year!

The Newton Isaac approach is for the lazy investor. One decision each year, usually accomplished with one phone call in early January, and the investment activity is complete. Obviously, the investor positioned in this mode isn't really concerned about the trend of the market. Most likely, in the year before a major market decline the worst performers will be precious metals and very conservative funds. At major market bottoms the dismal results will likely be found in high-tech and cyclical market segments. Thus at almost all times in almost all markets, at least one-third of the assets will be repositioned to next year's winners.

Those using technical market timing as the basic ongoing strategy may also be attracted to sector funds, particularly if the investor is hard-working and up to speed on sector performance.

At the timing-buy point, rather than using a conventional, broadly diversified general stock or growth fund—by definition, weighted to a variety of industries—this investor uses one or a few niche funds that either have performed most poorly in the decline, or represent an industry likely to rebound crisply because of economic or secular factors.

In the opinion of the authors, sector funds will be heavily represented with each passing year in both the top 10 percent of all fund performers, and also in the bottom 10 percent. The key questions for readers are:

1. Which would you prefer to own? Newton Isaac handles that simplistically.
2. Can the typical modest risk taker accept the price volatility inherent in this class or type of investment?

SECTOR FUNDS: A PRACTICAL USE

Putting aside our bias for broadly diversified funds, the sector and niche funds can play a significant part in the portfolios of both buy-and-hold investors and dollar-cost-averagers.

"Inflation rears its ugly head," say the headlines or underlying economic numbers. It is unlikely that a conventional stock or growth fund will move swiftly to weight the portfolio heavily in gold. Tax laws change, as they did in the early 1980s, to give a special benefit to the ownership of public utility stocks. "Uncle Sam Legislates Benefits for Drug Companies that Budget Heavily for Research," and so forth.

Since conventional fund management can move but gingerly, the investor reading profit into these specific industry-oriented situations can overweight the personal portfolio quickly by shifting 5–10 percent of assets to a precious metals, public utilities, or drug company intensive sector fund. If correct, the total return earned will be enhanced because the niche fund is a "pure play"—highly concentrated—whereas the generalized growth portfolio is a diluted play.

ENTER: VARIABLE & UNIVERSAL VARIABLE LIFE

The mutual fund family, particularly where investment and tax strategies are concerned, will never be the same! Since taxes, under the 1986 simplification legislation, will consume either 15 or 28 percent of earnings made from any investment strategy using conventional mutual funds held personally, the new VL and VUL policies are clearly the way to operate.

- These new investment options are really families of mutual funds sculpted within the confines of a life insurance contract.
- The tax collector is eliminated: no tax on income or gains, and none on transfers between the various investment options.
- Increasingly, these funds are offering sector funds as policy options: real estate, international portfolios, energy, junk bonds, and others.

Thus the asset allocation strategies discussed earlier—and particularly the timing of upswings and bear markets—are far more effective in the tax-deferring world of variable universal life than in the taxable world of the tax-naked conventional mutual fund.

The "D" series of strategies, "rebalancing," and almost any other investment approach will witness superior results in the

VL or VUL. After all, the 15–33 percent tax savings will usually cover all of the insurance company costs over time. Conversely, the management and tax costs associated with conventional funds will become tax form 1040 plagues in the new tax bill.

Every possibility from tried and proven buy-and-hold to a strategy as esoteric as "3-Dimensional" can be automatically executed in these new fund family offerings. The game of strategy using mutual funds can be as simple or complex as the investor can live with or design. The chapters on risk and reward and asset allocation should dictate that you are either a risk taker or not. The chapter covering tax-law changes will lead you either to a taxable fund, or to one of the new variable products. What's left? Your imagination, discipline, and hard work if complexity or simplicity is your game!

CHAPTER 6

MARKET TIMING— "AS EASY AS PI!"

Market timing of mutual funds is a complex and controversial subject for both investment professionals and fund shareholders. The markets are presumed by many top-notch experts to be *efficient*; which simply means that so much information is available simultaneously to all market participants that prices adjust automatically to the correct levels. Put another way, the market is efficient, while the market players are inefficient! If you experience the hoped-for big winner, market efficiency will likely follow the win with the unwanted loss that painfully balances the books.

Market timing is the technical discipline (commonly computer-based) that measures and attempts to evaluate the innards of the market to determine the major and minor trends—up, down and sideways. Market timing is the attempt to reverse the negative side of the efficient-market thesis. The truly successful timer could say, "My stock market always wins!"

What do technical market timers measure, what purpose do their studies serve, and why is this subject so relevant for mutual fund investors and variable insurance buyers?

Doubtless, there are thousands of things that the timer might measure where stocks, bonds, interest rates, and economic factors are considered. But, in general terms, the technicians focus on these key elements at work daily in the markets of stock and bonds:

- Volume of trading, and the composition of that volume. (Are more shares rising in price than declining? Is the relationship between rising prices and declining prices a trend that might be sustained?)

- Are more stocks reaching new highs or new lows? Again, is there a trend in the new high and low prices that could reflect a lasting direction for the markets?
- Is more money entering or leaving the stock market? If you add up the value of the shares rising in price versus those declining in price—mega-millions of calculations—the computer can gauge the money in and money out. Is there a discernible trend?
- Volume and price change in various classes of stocks. Are the blue chips getting the action, or is the trend toward cyclical issues, certain industry groups, or speculative stock groups?
- Are financial institutions—insurance companies, mutual funds, banks, investment counsel firms, and other "pros"—buying or selling shares? After all, the bulk of price movement these days is not a function of the average investor, but rather of these huge institutions.
- Odd-lot activity. The small buyer and seller of stocks is generally viewed as doing things backwards, buying with gusto when stocks are too high, and selling when stocks are really cheap.

The word for all this (including interest rates and the gross national/global product) is "econometric." The econometricians are market timers, and market timing may or may not be wonderful. After all, the basic premise of timing is that you can experience more than casual joy by being invested in a stock mutual fund when the trend is up, and earning interest in cash or bond funds when the stock trend is down. Nirvana? Possibly!

TIMING—WHY MUTUAL FUNDS AND VARIABLE LIFE POLICIES?

If the idea behind market timing is to be "in the market" when it is going up, and "out in cash" when it is in decline, then the modern mutual fund families—and the insurance proxies for them—are figuratively made in heaven. When the timers' device (called a "signal" in the trade) says the market is going up on a trend basis, switch cash fund or bond fund assets to the stock or growth fund within the same family (transaction cost, typically $5.00). When the timing signal says the market is headed south, reverse the above procedure.

While the sport fisherman fly casting for the fabled *Salmo salar* pays dearly for the opportunity, and the trader of stocks and bonds, even in a discount-brokerage world, pays a mean price to switch from "A" to "B", the mutual fund shareholder in the blockbuster modern fund family pays a pittance: usually $5.00, regardless of account or transfer size, and often nothing for the first few switches or changes each year. Consider this powerful economy when thinking about or contemplating mutual fund market timing:

- The professionally managed portfolio of securities (bond or stock) is already assembled. When the timer signals "in" or "out," the professionally selected portfolio is already in place and paid for!
- Unlike a short decade earlier, the array of funds that is available for timing purposes includes global, gold, specific geography, particular industry, and even funds that *time themselves*.

A clever clutch of new advisory services is now on the scene to help folks select, for example, the mutual fund family in which to invest; the correct timing for that family; and, believe or not, the precise sector of the stock, bond, or other market to be in! After all, "global" is a key Wall Street adjective these days, and "sector" is the hot noun in the mutual fund area. A June 1986 article in *Financial World* magazine estimated that some 500 market-timing money managers and related investment services were available. That number is surely higher today due to the growing number of sector fund advisories. Is there a less expensive alternative in market trading?

- The lowest cost you can find anywhere on Wall Street.

Switching between a sector fund and cash, or a growth fund and cash, is easily the cheapest out-of-pocket money deal in the whole financial world. Casting our fancy salmon and trout flies to fish that may never cooperate by rising is more expensive than trading millions of dollars in mutual fund shares.

The second advantage of timing using mutual funds is, again, cost.

- The $5.00 transaction cost from fund to fund is almost an unbelievable bargain of our time. However, the mutual fund itself is trading for a few pennies per share when portfolio assets are shifted from one investment to another. Every trade that the fund makes on your behalf as a shareholder saves real dollars in direct costs.

We have been aware since the mid-1960s of a few institutional, retirement plan, and college endowment funds that have timed millions of dollars using mutual funds. The results have been nothing short of spectacular in many cases, but in all events the cost of doing business has been at fire sale levels.

DOES MARKET TIMING REALLY WORK?

The market, for timing purposes, does only one thing: it fluctuates. The purpose of market timing is to separate up markets from downers. As a purely technical discipline, timing leaves guesswork and fundamental research to one set of analytical gnomes on the assumption that the supply-demand actions always at work on the trading desks really tell the whole story of up versus down. The other analytical gnomes, of course, ponder financial statements for their answers!

While many market timing firms exist today, many are far too new to be viewed conclusively in terms of proven results.

However, in June 1986, *Financial World* recorded the results actually delivered by nine important timing firms for the period 1/1/81 through 1/1/86. (See Figure 6–1.) This period is interesting since the market took some lumps during the double-digit inflation days, and then embarked on its subsequent powerful bull market.

And in March 1987, timing scorekeeper MoniResearch Corporation brought the scorecard up to date. (See Figure 6–2.) The

FIGURE 6–1
Time-Tested Rankings

Market Timer[1]	Annualized % Gain	Ending Value of Portfolio	Switches Per Year
Lincoln Inv. Planning	18.5	$23,393	3.0
J.D. Reynolds	16.7	21,617	4.4
R. Meeder & Assoc.	15.7	20,709	3.2[2]
Lowry Mgmt.	13.3	18,709	2.2
Smathers & Co.	13.2	18,581	3.0
Schabacker Invest. Mgmt.	11.5	17,233	4.6[2]
William Mason & Co.	11.3	17,061	5.6
Lipper Buy/Hold	11.3	17,061	0
Portfolio Mgmt. Svc.	10.8	16,708	3.2
T-Bill Buy/Hold	10.6	16,517	0
Shoal Berer	7.8	14,756	3.4

[1]From 1/1/81–1/1/86. 2. Buy/sells are not total; fractions of the portfolio are shifted back and forth between the aggressive and defensive mutual funds.

Source: Moni Research Corp., P.O. Box 19146, Portland, OR 97219, as printed in *Financial World*, June 1986.

market of stocks, after all, had been involved in massive fluctuation. . .and that is what timing is all about.

The benchmarks against which performance should be judged are the Lipper Buy/Hold and T-Bill Buy/Hold. Most of the timers studied above are well-known to the authors. Unfortunately, many not-so-wonderful timers are not included in this study. For some reason or other they—often the "unwonderful"—would not produce verified results. In other cases, the actual timing data was supplied only to financial institutions. In others, the data was not available for the entire period covered.

However, some important insights can be gleaned about market timing of mutual funds. First, timing can involve a very active trading environment (eleven trades in an average year for one timer), or fairly passive activity (with only one trades a year for another).

"Best results" do not appear to hinge on the number of transactions. The finest result—Lincoln Investment—resulted from 2.2 transactions a year, and the poorest from 3.2. Both are middle to bottom range in terms of frequency.

FIGURE 6–2
Performance Ranking

Group being ranked: Group A
Time period covered: 5 years, 2/5/82–2/5/87
Issue: March/April 1987

Market Timer	Annualized % Gain	Ending Value of Portfolio	Switches per Year	Notes
Lincoln Inv Planning	22.6	$27,728	2.2	
AFC Advisory Services	21.9	26,944	1.0	4.5
J. Reynolds	21.6	26,566	3.4	
Lipper Buy/Hold	21.0	25,987	0	3
Portfolio Timing	19.9	24,787	5.0	
R. Meeder Assoc	19.2	24,070	5.0	1
Zweig/Avatar	18.4	23,247	8.0	1
William Mason & Co.	16.8	21,743	4.6	
R. M. Leary & Co.	16.7	21,647	5.0	4
Lowry Management Corp	16.4	21,358	2.6	
Schabacker Inv. Mgmt.	15.8	20,909	4.4	1
Koyen, Clarke & Co.	15.7	20,759	11.0	4
Portfolio Mgmt Serv	15.1	20,246	2.6	
Shoal Berer	11.7	17,381	3.2	
Money Mkt Buy/Hold	9.1	15,456	0	3
T-Bill Buy/Hold	8.8	15,268	0	3

Source: MoniResearch Corp., P.O. Box 19146, Portland, OR 97219.

The key observation, since results are everything, is that market timing of mutual funds can either be a whole lot better than a buy-and-hold strategy, or much less productive.

A simple arithmetic exercise tied to the methodology of market timing can be helpful to you at this point. First, nobody really ever sells at the precise market top or buys at the actual market bottom. After all, daily price swings of more than one hundred points for the Dow Jones Industrials are now a matter of record. The bottom and top are not the issue, but the trend and the duration and extent of these are of value. Thus the timers' dream is to avoid 70 percent of a major trend decline, and to be fully invested in stock or growth funds for 70 percent of a bull trend.

Do the humble numbers in Figure 6–3 tell the whole story? Maybe! Here, successful market timing produced a "total return"

FIGURE 6–3
The Arithmetic of Timing Profit

Invested for the desired rise	70%
In cash for the bear trend	70%
Percentages totaled	140%

Source: Andersen & Walsh, Inc.

result equal to 140 percent of the average of all typical stock market investors. Inspecting the *Financial World* presentation (Figure 6–1), the conservative T-Bill Buy/Hold, if timed, should be worth a 14.8 percent annualized return. The more aggressive Lipper Buy/Hold investor, if timed, should have expected annualized returns of 15.8 percent.

Since timers charge a fee for providing the signals, only three of those presented in Figure 6–1—Lincoln, Reynolds, and Meeder—proved worthy of their fee! Even Lowry, once considered the premier timer, could not pass muster when the chips—your fund investments—were on the timing table.

Does market timing of mutual funds work? Of course it does, if you happened to have select Lincoln as the timer. . .or their new timed mutual fund, The Rightime Fund. Does it always work? Of course not! Three of the eight timers did not better the buy-and-hold scenario for stock funds, and one fell distantly behind the zero-risk exposure offered by Treasury bills!

Thus if we extrapolate over the growing list of more than five hundred timers of mutual funds, variable insurance products, or market indices, one-third are worth the management fee, one-third are marginal—like Lowry and Smathers—and one-third are dismal. Yet most market timers charge roughly the same fee for their services in rendering timing advice to clients (typically 2 percent of assets under management each year).

IS THERE A TIME FOR TIMING?

Mutual fund managers, particularly those that operate with a growth or speculative investment objective, despise timing and shareholders who switch frequently. Here is why:

1. Fund managers tend to be serious, well-educated folks, running portfolios for serious long-term investors. The sudden shock of huge sums entering or leaving their fund is, at best, disconcerting.
2. Among the well-educated and experienced class of investor, a sincere belief exists that great investments are picked on the basis of fundamentals—earnings, cash flows, dividends, book values, etc.—not from an evaluation of stock trends.
3. The timer is a cheat. Selling at a fixed price after the exchanges have closed, the timer saddles the "good investor"—Mr. and Ms. Buy & Hold—with all of those expensive transaction costs. After all, when the timer moves from the growth, stock, or sector fund to cash, the portfolio manager usually incurs commission expense to raise the cash required for payment.

From the perspective of the investor, timing works wonderfully at certain times, and dismally at others. When the stock or bond markets are in a large uptrend—as from mid-August of 1982 to date—timing tends to work poorly, particularly if the timing is sensitive to short-range data. Lowry, in the *Financial World* study, was once king of the long market cycle. Clients today wonder. The timing experience for them in this mega-bull trend has been at least *horrible*. And Lowry, if you refer to the rankings in Figure 6–1, has the lowest transaction velocity in the timing group (2.2 switches per year).

Timing will always have an obvious place in the minds of investors, planners, and brokers. However, if the market is in a major bull trend, or the reverse, being on the correct side will rarely augur well for timers—Lincoln is one exception, and BASIC is another. The problem is simple. How does the timer adjust for an Ivan Boesky or a Martin Siegel? How does the timer adjust to the new world of financial instruments such as options, index options, options on options, futures on options, options on futures, and the dazzling array of new trading instruments? It looks a lot like an angler's flybox: hundreds of feathery objects with dozens of hook sizes, some lures designed to float and others to sink, some for sunny weather and others for use at dusk.

Yes. . .market timing works well with mutual funds. But, some caveats:

- The time (in terms of the markets themselves) must be appropriate. Timing of funds seems to work its wonders best when markets are engaged in short-term swings rather than extended robust engagements with powerful tops and bottoms.
- Every new statistical notion begets a horde of new market timers, as did the "hemline" approach, and the "sun spot" theories of the past. One-third will win and deserve the management fee, while the others will be underperformers. Whatever they charge will be an outrageous price!

Market timing of mutual funds in the modern mutual fund family is more discipline and strategy than an investment technique. It is a conservative strategy: being out of the market during a precipitous decline is far more important than being invested in the market when it is rising. A classic example is Hartford's BASIC Timing. In Figure 6–4, we see that BASIC has missed much of the important upswing during 1985 and 1986. Yet on a long-term basis the service has performed significantly better than the market itself. The reason? Declines were avoided.

MENTAL PITFALLS

The disciplines involved in timing are purely technical and statistical. The financial news of the moment, political turmoil on the front pages, and pronouncements about the economy or markets by sage political and economic figures play no role in the timing game.

Stock and bond fundamentals must be totally disregarded for timing to be a productive investment strategy. The majority of great timing signals usually occur when the media is telling a quite different story.

Harry O. Kline, a senior sales officer with the Franklin Group of funds, and possibly the most knowledgeable person about timing in the mutual fund industry, has compiled a folio

FIGURE 6–4
Basic Market Timing vs. the S&P 500 Index

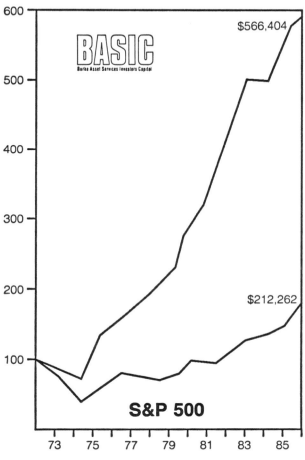

Source: Basic, Inc. Hartford, CT 06103

of financial publication covers dating over nearly three decades. These covers tell the story:

- "Experts Say Bull Market to Continue"
- "Economy Registering Powerful Gains"
- "Dividend Increases and Stock Splits At Record Pace"

These, or similar pronouncements, were usually coincident with major sell signals preceding large stock market declines, 1973–74 representing a classic example. Conversely, "No End To The Bear Market In Sight" generally coincided with a terrific buy signal.

Thus if you have retained a market timer or timing service, it is probably best to cancel your subscriptions to investment tabloids, and take front-page headlines with a grain of salt. These, it appears, have little to do with the technical underpinnings of the stock market, and tend to derail successful timing.

Market timing is also a long-range affair. Once it is embraced as the desired strategy, and the appropriate mutual fund group is selected, the investor should commit to at least a full market cycle: five years or longer.

> Kline's Law says, "Any investor, over any period of time, who can avoid one precipitous market decline, will do twice as well as all other investors."

In the 1970s, for example, avoiding 1974 by being on the cash side of that devastating decline would have roughly doubled total returns earned, if the investor had stayed invested in a good stock or growth fund for the balance of the decade! Thus timing requires time to work its wonders. The majority of investors who have both timed funds and bad memories did not give the strategy enough time to deliver that one victory: in cash, earning interest, while the market of stocks tumbled.

THE WHIPSAW

Timing sounds so wonderful—money in a stock fund when the market is going up, and safe in cash when the market is in decline. We have already worked the arithmetic of timing, showing that if the investor can get 70 percent participation up and avoid 70 percent down, the result will be a clear investment victory. However, along the way there will be whipsaws, and these can be expensive and frustrating.

A whipsaw occurs when the timing signal interprets the market to be changing direction, shifts the timed assets to the flip side—from the growth fund to cash fund, for example—and the market continues to rise, forcing the timer back into equities at a higher price. Or, the timer records a buy signal, shifts cash to the growth fund, and the market continues lower, generating a shift back to cash and simultaneously recording a loss of capital, often a large one!

It is best to expect that the first series of transactions will include one or more whipsaws. Expecting early error will strengthen resolve. Not expecting the whipsaw has typically caused the investor to quit timing in disgust just before a correct series of signals is generated.

And, of course, there is the question of cost. Modern portfolio theory says you cannot consistently beat the market. The decision to adopt a timing strategy means, by definition, that the investor will be attempting to disprove the efficient-market hypothesis in two ways. Both of these involve costs that are not present when measuring actual investment results against stock averages, which are free from commission and management fees:

- The fund group selected may have a loan or sales charge, and the fund will be charging a management fee (which is often larger than 1 percent a year).
- The timing service or advisory selected will assess a charge as well. This charge may be in the form of a management fee—2 percent is typical—or a subscription to a service that may range from a few hundred dollars a year to a thousand dollars or so.

With those continuing expenses in place—in sum, perhaps 3 percent for a $50,000 account—the "bogey" to beat the S&P 500 has been increased quite a lot. If the S&P 500 has averaged roughly 11 percent for the previous 50 years, the timed account must average 14 percent simply to break even!

So now implementation of a market-timing discipline for a mutual fund involves the dreaded whipsaw (a form of cost in that the stock or growth fund itself would produce better results since it did not whipsaw); and a set of out-of-pocket costs that must be overcome to deliver actual results superior to those generated by the unmanaged, commission-free market averages.

WHO SHOULD TIME?

Prior to passage of the 1986 tax legislation, the standard answer was that timing should be restricted to tax-deferred accounts such as qualified retirement plans and endowed funds.

This reasoning stemmed from the nature and frequency of signal generation. The discipline requires that action be taken immediately when the timing signal is flashed. Under previous tax rules involving a specific holding period to record a long-term capital gains exposure, the signals invariably came too soon. Thus the taxable timing investor was subject to higher taxes, or attempted to wait for the magic date only to find that a significant and negative price effect had occurred as well!

With the new lower maximum tax rates, taxable accounts might consider market timing as a reasonable alternative to the conventional buy-and-hold scenario. However, the life insurance industry has recently provided a remarkable vehicle that can eliminate the tax question entirely for an individual's normally taxable assets: the variable life and universal variable life insurance policy.

These vehicles, which we will deal with in-depth elsewhere, do not generate a form 1099 or summary of transactions for the tax man! Thus the variable contract with a good equity vehicle—Western Reserve Life with Janus Management as the manager, for example—and a cash fund or high-quality bond fund in the same policy, becomes a first-class timing vehicle. No current tax on dividend or interest income, and no current tax on transfers between the policy investment vehicles, creates a new world of tax-avoidance for creative market timing.

BASIC, timing the Janus Fund as a taxable series of transactions, would have produced a tax disaster for the pre-1987 taxable account. However, since Janus is a clone vehicle in the universal variable policy offered by Western Reserve Life, the timer can have the best of both worlds: a very fine growth manager, and no current liability for capital gains or income tax.

TIMING SECTOR FUNDS

Fidelity boasts in the media that they have "reinvented the stock market," and in a sense they have. Their sector or specific industry funds cover virtually every market segment. Putnam Funds, the Vanguard group, and other fund sponsors are also busily crafting new funds to deal with specific market areas.

To this point we have been dealing with fund timing entirely on the basis of the broad market as represented by the Dow, S&P, and other major market indices. The fast-growing list of sector funds provides a whole new dimension for the world of timing by timing both the major trends, but selecting specific industry funds for implementation when the signal says "buy."

Investment newsletters offering sector strategies are flourishing. Since these publications have not been in print through a full market cycle, it isn't realistic to even attempt to comment on their effectiveness. However, if market timing based on the major indices can enhance total returns, timing using the correct sector funds could produce returns ranging from incredible to fantastic!

Each year and each major market shift produces changed leadership. In recent years, property & casualty stocks, broadcast and media issues, the telecommunications group, and even brokerage stocks themselves have played leadership roles at various times. Their recorded results on the upside have been a multiple of the price increases registered by the market averages. Thus, armed with a buy signal, and being positioned in these sector funds for the successful upswing, would mean results equal to a multiple of the timing multiple! However, this timing approach is hardly for the faint of heart, or those with queasy digestive systems!

BRAND NEW: TIMING FUNDS

One of the larger historic problems in successfully timing the markets using mutual funds (with the possible exception of the fully invested Keystone stock funds) was the ever-present fear that a good buy signal would produce underperformance because the growth or stock fund selected was heavily in cash. To put it another way, the fund manager was not bullish. Thus, a correct signal could produce mediocre returns.

It is not unusual to see funds labeled as growth vehicles even though they are 30 percent to 50 percent in cash or defensive securities when the market is well into a growth phase. As noted earlier, most mutual funds are managed by fundamentalists, not technicians.

Thus, as the 1980s reached its mid-point, a new class of mutual fund began to emerge: a fund operated by market timers that timed the underlying portfolio. The Lowry Fund came first, followed by the Portfolio Series, Flex-Fund, Greenwich Monitrend, and Rightime Fund.

In most cases these funds time the market using common stocks or options on them when in a buy mode, shifting to cash or "put" options against portfolio holdings when on the sell side. Financial and index futures also are used at times as hedging tools.

The Rightime Fund is a notable exception. Rightime, when bullish, uses other stock and growth funds as the implementation tools. . .and selects these funds based on "positive alpha." In this approach, the fund must be delivering returns superior to those suggested by its risk exposure, or "beta." The Rightime Fund presently has more than 40 stock and growth funds in its portfolio.

In the cases of the five funds with positive alpha (see Figure 6–5), the annual management fee is obviously well-earned. Con-

FIGURE 6–5
5 Funds with Positive Alpha and 5 with Negative Alpha

Mutual Funds with Good Alpha, A Sample		
FUND	*BETA*	*ALPHA*
Amev Capital	1.11	7.09
Kemper Technology	1.24	3.60
Keystone K-2	.93	4.66
Mathers	1.05	4.37
Phoenix Balanced	.72	2.79
. . . and, Negative Alpha		
Dreyfus Fund	.81	−2.65
Fidelity Freedom	1.32	−8.78
Keystone S-3	1.24	−4.97
Oppenheimer Fund	1.28	−9.49
Sequoia	.64	−9.16

Source: Rightime Econometrics

versely, for those funds that are performing poorly relative to the beta risk, the management fee is money spent poorly. The Rightime Fund folks, measuring alpha and beta for hundreds of funds on a weekly basis, take a lot of guesswork out of the fund selection game. The fund buys winning managers, not the ever-present second and third best.

As we view the world of timing—despite the dismal performance recorded to date by the Lowry entry—the timing funds present the most efficient methodology for timing. These are hands-on, full-time managers, a point with powerful implications.

Some years ago a midwestern broker with a significant timing clientele was mountain-climbing in Asia. His instructions and related client documentation was in a desk drawer at his home. He had not left the keys at his office. A timing signal was generated! Since he was not reachable for a number of days, the losses mounted.

With these new timing funds, that disastrous possibility is automatically avoided. The manager is full-time, and the manager can usually make portfolio alterations in a matter of minutes; in the case of Rightime, in seconds!

Our favorite among the timing funds would be Rightime, even though the 12b-1 and management fees look a bit rich on the surface. Our reasoning stems from the *Financial World* and Moni Research studies noted earlier. Rightime is sponsored by Lincoln Investment the fund that produced the best returns in the 1981–86 market cycle and was fully invested for growth when the huge bull market move was at hand in early 1987.

Can we arrive at any concrete conclusions based on our experience with timing and timers, or our years of observing the procedure in action? As the *Financial World* article notes, "It's so easy: Make money during rallies and preserve it during declines. Alas, market timers aren't quite so predictable."

- First, the investor must come to grips with the reality of timing, the risks and foibles, and the mental discipline that's required.
- Next, the investor must be sanguine that the added costs of timing can be overcome. Mediocre timing plus that additional 3 percent is potentially a heavy burden on total return.

- And then, the correct fund group to time (or timing fund to employ) must be selected; and where a fund family is chosen, the source of timing signals must be hired.
- If the asset to be managed is a qualified retirement plan including participants who are not owner-employees, there is the added question of investment prudence.

As Nick Forst, president of Lincoln Investment notes, "The entire timing concept is built on safety—how safe we can be at reduced risk." In Lincoln's case (and so far it is also true for its Rightime Fund), the prudence of timing is documented. But for others in the timing world, the returns delivered versus the unmanaged indices would hardly make a prudent man smile.

However, as long as the market of stocks traverses peaks and valleys, and market technicians search for new things to measure in that market, timing of mutual funds will continue to be a serious force in the investment world.

CHAPTER 7

TAX CHANGES: NO HELP FOR THE FUND INVESTOR

"When everybody has got money they cut taxes, and when they're broke they raise 'em. That's statesmanship of the highest order."

Will Rogers, 1929

WIN OR LOSE, TAXES HAVE INDEED BEEN CHANGED!

The comprehensive tax revisions signed into law in 1986 (to be implemented in the 1987–90 period) may have been referred to in the press as "tax simplification," but for investors subject to tax, on dividends, interest income, and capital gains, the new bill offers nothing but problems and potential pitfalls.

Readers have likely been deluged with mail from banks, financial planners, brokerage firms, and even tax preparers offering booklets and seminars purporting to explain the new bill. Newspapers and magazines have run countless articles on the subject, and, as we are writing, three books about the bill are on the best-seller list in the Sunday *New York Times*!

In spite of all the hoopla and commotion, much is still to be learned about the 1986 Tax Reform Act. Regulations and interpretations are likely to flow from Washington like a salmon river in spate until this tax act, like all other tax acts before it, is replaced by still another tax bill. And, in the interim, the courts and private-sector accounting/tax/legal community will battle the heady issues extant in the tax world.

For the record, tax changes seem to occur almost every year:

- 1968: Prepaid interest rules were changed.
- 1969: General tax reform.
- 1970: Constructive interest rules were revised and rates on these rose to 12 percent.
- 1975: The tax reduction act.
- 1976: The tax reform act.
- 1977: The tax reduction and simplification act (sound familiar?).
- 1978: The revenue act of 1978.
- 1980: The installment sales revision act.
- 1981: The economic recovery act.
- 1982: The tax equity and fiscal responsibility act.
- 1984: Tax reform act of that year.
- 1985: Flat tax and simplicity gain momentum again.

Then, in 1986, the bombshell: The Internal Revenue Service Act. Readers will note that this legislation, unlike much of that prior to it, was named after the IRS. Obviously Congress did not want to take the public heat, whose source we shall reveal as we move forward.

REALITY NOW

Our focus here is to explore the known elements of tax simplification as they affect the present and future investor in mutual funds; aware as we write that somewhere in Washington a word processor is busily at work on revisions to the bill recently enacted, or drafting a new proposal that will eliminate, replace, or largely revise the shape of the taxpayers' ball field.

Tongue in cheek, the new bill suggested to the taxpayers of America that life would be simple. The proposed form 1040 in Figure 7–1 makes jest of that assertion, as does the hubbub created by the Internal Revenue Service's issuance of its form W-4 for withholding—a form so complex as to be confusing even for the skilled tax preparer.

FIGURE 7–1
The Simplified Form 1040

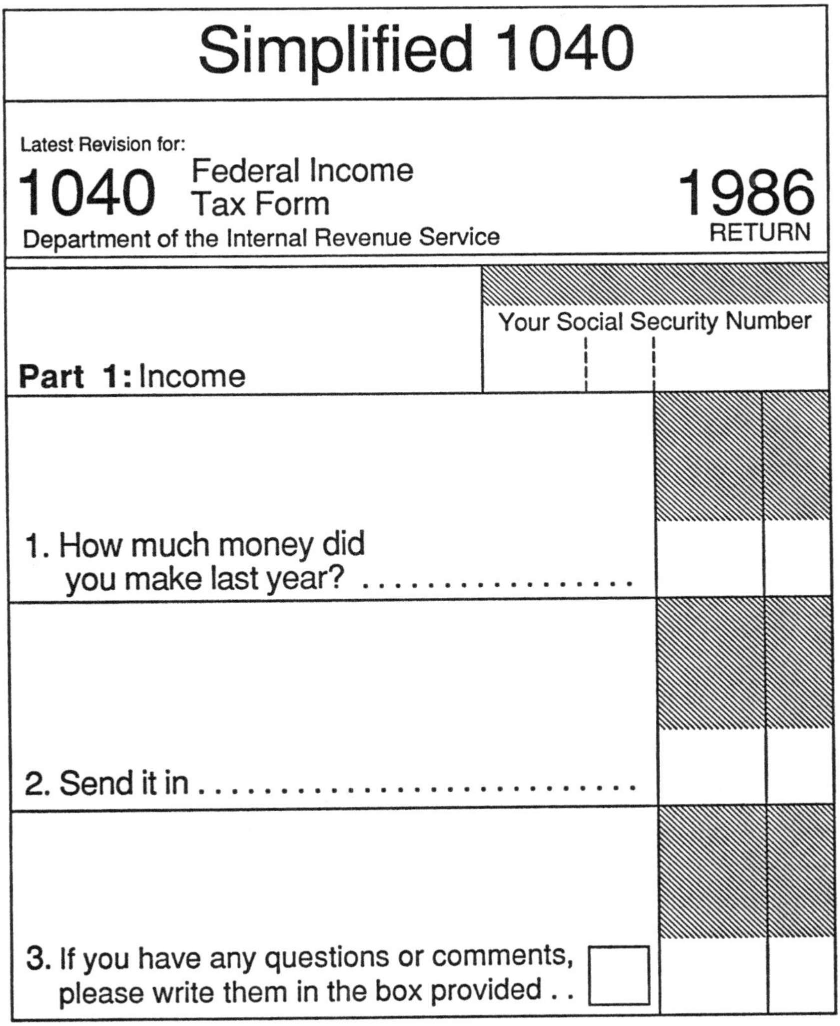

Simplified 1040

Latest Revision for:

1040 Federal Income
Tax Form

Department of the Internal Revenue Service

1986
RETURN

Your Social Security Number

Part 1: Income

1. How much money did
   you make last year? . . . .

2. Send it in . . . .

3. If you have any questions or comments,
   please write them in the box provided . .

Source: Internal Revenue Service

"An income tax is like a laundry list—either way you lose your shirt."

Fred Allen, 1954

The year 1954 was the last time the entire tax payment system was revised, top to bottom. The 1986 bill is a complete reworking of that graduated format, riddled as it was with more than two decades of lobbying and Congressional tinkering. Mr. Allen, then in the final days of an immortal career in radio, hit the button squarely on the head.

A well worn adage in investment and financial planning has it that "nothing is sure but death and taxes . . . but death doesn't get worse every year!" For investors in mutual funds—other than those sheltered by qualified retirement plans such as pensions or IRAs—the new tax bill indeed represents less benevolent and more confusing exposures than its predecessor.

TAX CHANGE: NO BARGAIN FOR MUTUAL FUND INVESTORS

Yes, if the promise of the bill comes true, rates payable on dividends and interest earned through fund ownership will drop to a maximum level of 38.5 percent in 1987, and in 1988 to (presumably) flat rates of 15 percent or 28 percent. However, the 15 percent rate applies only to incomes under $29,750 for joint returns, and a paltry $17,850 for single individuals. Those penny-pinching income levels sound very close to the poverty line.

Studies of income levels for mutual fund shareholders would likely find actual, reportable taxable incomes considerably higher than $30,000. Calls to a number of mutual fund sponsors on this topic provided little definitive data, though the guesses on average shareholder incomes ranged from $32,000 to $45,000. So, most mutual fund investors are likely to be in the higher bracket if the heady tax simplification promise of 1988 is kept. Doubtful? You bet!

DEATH TO THE IRA

The most widely discussed change in the bill relates to the Individual Retirement Account (IRA). A *New York Times* article in February 1987 estimated that one-third of all families participate in this "Ambitious Savings Experiment." And further:

- Assets in existing IRA accounts had grown to more than $300 billion; and
- More than 11 percent of these assets were invested in mutual fund shares.

We believe that the number of dollars is probably far greater than $300 billion. It is quite likely that the market share for mutual funds is now closer to 15 percent. Falling interest rates at savings institutions, commercial banks, and other thrifts have swept both existing IRA accumulations and new contributions toward brokerage firms, mutual funds, and other riskier investments.

But the wonderful IRA—deductible contributions coupled with tax-deferred accumulation of dividends, interest, and gains— is dead for most readers, at least in terms of the prized deduction of new contributions. You may continue to contribute to your IRA and get some or all of the important previous tax benefits if:

- You earn under $25,000 (filing singly) or $40,000 (filing a joint return).
- You are not an active participant in a company or employer-sponsored sheltered retirement plan.

These earnings limitations also reduce the number of qualified IRA households by a possible 50 percent. Since there are more than one million qualified employer-sponsored retirement plans, the remaining 50 percent is likely halved again. Thus the vaunted IRA for retirement has been relegated to the legions that probably cannot afford to make the ongoing contributions, or will contribute to investment and savings options that have little lustre.

So the promise of a better retirement for millions of American families vanishes in the measured world of tax reform circa 1986. The thoughtful notion that a supplement to the seemingly shaky Social Security System was a logical people and political concept simultaneously bites the proverbial dust! And this useful tool that was working to make our profligate society a thrifty one again is put in mothballs . . . like the fabled Packard, Auburn, and Cord motorcars that once made driving in America wonderful!

For those millions now using mutual funds for existing IRA accumulations, the news remains great. The modern family of funds is the ideal repository for IRA investment, handily providing more flexibility and total-return potential than any other option, with the possible exception of the self-directed IRA accounts offered through both conventional and discount brokerages, and bank trust departments.

The key question posed to those who have become accustomed to making the regular $2,000 contribution, or the additional "spousal" $250, is whether or not to continue on a nondeductible tax basis. After all, even though the continued contribution will not result in the treasured immediate tax savings, Uncle Sam still allows the dividends and other earnings to accumulate on a favored, tax-postponed basis.

Our guess, for most families, is that new contributions would best be directed elsewhere. Tax-exempt bond funds provide one workable solution for those seeking a low-risk, tax-free option. Another option is the new variable life and universal variable life contracts that now offer a free-standing family of mutual funds looking much like insurance. In the case of these variable insurance contracts, both the risk avoider and those seeking growth can be served.

The reasoning here stems from a single word: liquidity. The IRA is a truly restricted asset. Withdrawals from accumulations in these accounts before age 59½ are penalized. And assets in the IRA cannot be used as collateral for a loan. Thus liquidity is seriously hampered if the rules are violated.

Conversely, the tax-exempt bond fund provides instant liquidity in some cases through check-writing privileges, and five-day liquidity in the conventional municipal bond fund or unit trust. And all interest income earned by investing in these mutuals is accumulating and compounding tax-free, which is clearly better for the investor than mere tax postponement—other things equal.

The variable or variable universal insurance contract also provides the liquidity discussed earlier, though there are some limitations that will be dealt with in later chapters. These insurance investment-linked policies also provide for tax deferral of all current income, and at the death of the named insured—as you will see in Chapter 8—virtual income-tax freedom.

However, the variable contracts also offer the other element important to the accumulation of wealth: flexibility. Typically, these policies will offer at least a money market, bond, balanced fund, and stock or growth fund option. Thus the previous IRA saver using this approach has tax freedom plus liquidity and flexibility. Why is liquidity so important?

- The family may have pre-college children. Tuition costs are skyrocketing. The IRA account, as noted earlier, is a terribly expensive source of funds for this purpose.
- A new or larger home, or a vacation villa may be a goal. The IRA asset is unavailable either to fund the deposit, or as collateral for the mortgage loan. Some friends of the authors, without advice, recently used their IRA assets for a home purchase. Needless to say, that act increased the cost of home ownership by quite a lot!
- A serious long-term illness that over-runs the medical policy limits requires large amounts of cash. Does the IRA provide these very high-cost funds? The answer may well be yes, but the penalties and charges for early withdrawal will require some aspirin at tax time.

A chapter-length list of reasons to avoid non-deductible IRA contributions is reasonably possible. However, the three listed above highlight the largest issues likely to confront the family circumstance. But the vanishing IRA is hardly the most significant impact in the larger world of mutual funds and tax change. As fisherman Weeks might rightly observe, "The fish are in the water, and the fly is tied on the line, but the fishin' is gettin' tougher every time out!"

THE DEVILS IN THAT SIMPLE BILL!

Yes, the maximum tax bracket is going down to 28 percent (unless the taxpayer is subject to the AMT—Alternative Minimum Tax calculation). That's the good news. But bad news and tax devils abound in this era of taxation, called "simplification" by some and "reduction" by others. Be reminded of the list of previous tax bills earlier in the chapter.

For example, while the maximum tax exposure reduces to 28 percent for earned income, dividends, and interest, the rate payable on capital gains rises to equal that heady number. Previously, this rate on realized capital gains was levied at one-half the taxpayer's bracket rate, or 20 percent, if the gains were long-term in nature—six months under some earlier tax bills, and one year under the terms of others.

Since managed mutual funds by definition trade portfolio assets—some of them quite actively—there will be capital gains (or losses). Many of the great growth and stock funds (and today the "sector" funds) erode most of the dividend income in the management and expense process, but deliver big capital gains payments to the shareholder. These, of course, are now 40 percent more expensive on the new form 1040! And, as we will see in pages ahead, more evil tax devils will surface that can cause harm, increase costs, and further add to U.S. taxpayers' aspirin consumption!

To make the taxable capital gains story come home to roost in terms of past and present tax levels, review the mutual funds listed in Figure 7–2.

BEDEVILED AGAIN

Taking the Individual Retirement Account away is one serious thing, and increasing the tax gobble on capital gains is another. However, we are only at the proverbial "tip of the iceberg" at this point. That the new tax bill accomplishes its advertised simplicity is arguable when we reach for the balance of the tax menu for mutual funds and shareholders.

FIGURE 7–2
1986: Ten Funds with Big Gains Paid and Taxed

Fund	Price 12/31/86	Capital Gains Distributed	Percent
Acorn	$37.08	$6.07	16.4
Axe Houghton B	11.10	2.78	25.0
Bull & Bear Cap. Growth	10.37	5.91	56.9
Cigna Growth	12.91	3.52	27.3
Chemical Fund	6.87	3.13	45.6
Delaware Fund	18.34	4.31	23.5
Dreyfus Fund	10.50	2.60	24.8
Founders Mutual	7.87	2.59	32.9
Inv. Co. of America	13.19	2.45	18.6
Mathers Fund	16.69	7.38	43.52

A devil of preposterous size surfaces immediately in "simplification." In this case, the devil is really a phantom. The phantom creeps into the mutual fund domain much like a family of termites invades a luxurious and elegant wooden structure: always at work, but generally invisible to the human eye until the end is near.

The phantom today relates to a significant change in the tax treatment of management fees and expenses by the mutual fund itself. Operating under previous tax bills, the fund or funds you owned paid the management and related costs as a corporation or trust. The mutual funds then typically offset these charges against dividend or interest income actually received by the fund. The result, on your tax return, was a non-event: the fund itself earned income that was not taxable to you as a fund shareholder, and it used this income to expense the costs of operation and management of the fund or funds. How cute! How simple! The mutual fund family did the complicated stuff, while the fund shareowner basked in the heaven of tax freedom and simplicity.

The folks in Washington who make the rules evidently thought it was *too* cute. Under the new rules the funds will now pass the expenses of management through to the fund shareholder. This tax phantom—the flowing through of taxable income that does not involve the flow of real spendable or investable money—is now the source of the dreaded "phantom income" embedded in our simpler new tax return. Refer again to the string of yearly tax alterations in the tax patch. Nothing in Washington ever gets simpler. As Albert Einstein once noted, "The hardest thing in the world to understand is the income tax."

Here is how you will see it in the flesh. The statement from the mutual fund will insist that you were credited with dividends and interest earnings worth X dollars, and capital gains amounting to Y dollars. But the figure on your tax form 1099 will equal Z dollars, a number somewhat larger than the actual combination of income and gains. That is phantom income, and it is a psychological and practical bogey-man in the 1986 tax bill. Here's how:

- Income taxes due on income never received is something quite different for the typical U.S. taxpayer. Usually only the aggressive tax-shelter buyer was forced to contend with this problem.
- Income tax liability—the transfer of the fund manager's expenses to the fund holder—must be written down on long-form 1040, using a complex and difficult set of rules.

The slogan in 1776 was, "No taxation without representation." Our "simplified" tax act will likely result in a different and more painful slogan, "Representation, yes. Taxes, yes. Income to keep, no!" Fisherfriend Weeks, around for quite a time (but not that long), reflects that the new tax bill is no "Tea Party!"

We find it interesting that in reviewing a half-dozen tax booklets prepared by larger financial institutions—tax preparers, banks, and the venerable Commerce Clearing House (an important tax advisory service)—we found that the various indices did not once include mutual funds, nor did the content's pages. Yet phantom income lives, and the greatest of tax devils results from that life.

ALTERNATIVE MINIMUM TAX

If there exists a single line in the jargon of modern taxation that strikes fear in the hearts of tax preparers and tax owners alike, it is clearly "the Alternative Minimum Tax," adjoined to "you are subject to it!" The legislation forces AMT on millions of additional families, and mutual funds often play a key role in this more than dismal and often costly event.

The Alternative Minimum Tax, as the reader has gathered, is bad news. The tax is a "win-win" for the Treasury, and a "lose-lose" for taxpayers. AMT requires that you first calculate taxes according to the published tax tables. Then, adding back certain types of previously non-taxed income, or reversing previously legitimate deductions, you or your tax preparer must recalculate the liability to Uncle Sam and pay the higher amount.

The phantom-income issue will tend to exacerbate the dreaded AMT result. The AMT will work its doleful result on a mutual fund investor, particularly one who is in a tax-exempt or municipal bond trust or fund. AMT-triggered taxes can only rise for millions of mutual fund shareholders.

Since the amount of phantom income owed as a result of fund ownership will not be known until the fund reports to shareholders in the subsequent tax year, there is no early or timely opportunity for the taxpayer to make adjustments. This negative window could result in serious tax penalties for underpayment, stingy withholding, or underestimating. In a flash of AMT magic, the good guys become the bad guys!

Good guys, in the context of AMT, are also the humble savers and investors in America. These folks who keep the economic system alive by saving and investing might better be called the saviors. Time will tell.

Measuring on the basis of income taxation only, the mutual fund industry took a significant negative hit in the 1986 tax revision.

- Capital gains taxes increased 40 percent.
- Management expenses will be transferred to the fund shareholder rather than being expensed by the fund management.
- Even very small shareholders in mutual funds may now be exposed to the Alternative Minimum Tax.

And, the IRA is history for many of America's families. Treasure the IRA assets you have in place, as Uncle Sam likely paid for one-half. These money balances are compounding like Jack's beanstalk or Weeks' spawning salmon if they are in a bank or thrift savings account, or quite a bit faster if you are among the one in six who purchased mutual funds and the modern fund family to enhance that elusive search for "high total return."

FUND FAMILIES VERSUS VARIABLE LIFE

Whereas the tax-exposed mutual fund investor comes through simplification as a clear loser, the insurance investor emerges as the absolute winner. The lucky and incisive variable insurance policy holders will likely become tomorrow's wealthy Americans.

The variable life (VL) or universal variable life (VUL) holder, as opposed to the taxable fund holder, does not watch his or her mailbox in mid-to-late January for tax form 1099 to arrive. Under present tax rules, the life insurers offering VLs and VULs do not send, and are not required to send—1099s to the policy holder or the Internal Revenue Service. For the moment, variable insurance products are clearly where the tax action is!

Thus the tax simplification act of 1986 might be referred to as tax wreckage. Mutual fund shareholders clearly lost the battle. Life insurance companies—at least those that moved swiftly to the variable offerings that will be discussed in the two subsequent chapters—clearly won the war.

However, this book is not written about taxes. The game herein is clearly one of investment strategy and proper financial planning. Taxes do play a key role since investment returns must really be reduced to a net number: what was earned after taxes were paid and inflation was adjusted out of the gross number credited. That percentage—adjusted total return—is found in Figure 7–3.

Thus, taxes and inflation at present levels account for almost one-half of the gross return. Since the major blue chip stock averages have produced results nearly five full percentage points lower than the 15 percent used above, net investment return would run around 4 percent. For buyers of bank certificates of deposit and money market fund holders, the actual return would be between one and two percent.

So, while taxes are not the premier element in investment thinking, they certainly play a major role. And the new legis-

FIGURE 7–3
Total Investment Return Adjusted

Gross Income/Gains Earned	15.0%
Less:	
Taxes paid at 28%	(4.2%)
Inflation	(3.0%)
Equals Net Investment Return	7.8%

lation certainly has not helped much. We are, it seems, in a major bull market for stocks. Interest rates have been halved or more in recent years. Dividend levels—the income most heavily taxed before—have been declining as stock prices have advanced (more than a doubling for the larger indices in just a few years).

Thus while the potential tax on dividends and interest income has declined in the new bill, the tax on capital gains, (the key game in a major stock market rally) has been increased. As a result, many market gurus and advisors counsel that investors should be owning income-oriented mutual funds. However, the income on these is clearly declining as the stock market rises!

Tax questions should be the final consideration for investors and savers. First come the critical questions:

- What is your risk tolerance? (Use the "Rule of 6" or other software for this most important question).
- How should the assets be allocated among the major investment choices available in the selected mutual fund family? (The Sass/Southmark "Beta*Calc" software could be useful and instructive in this exercise).
- Which investment strategy best suits your investment objective? Are you "buy-and-hold", for example, or do the more esoteric ideas embraced in the "D" series seem to fit?

Once these are dealt with to your satisfaction, and the proper fund family is discovered (we will deal with that issue in depth in Chapter 10) you can decide the tax question in realistic terms.

The alternative to paying taxes—the variable insurance contracts—may be the answer if taxes loom as a very large issue. With that in mind, we push into the relatively new world of these variable products.

CHAPTER 8

THE EVERYMAN TAX SHELTER

"Thrift is the great fortune-maker. It draws the line between the savage and the civilized man."

Andrew Carnegie, 1900

LIFE INSURANCE INDUSTRY DOES ITS THING WITH GUSTO!

The salmon in Ted Weeks' fabled rivers have done exactly the same thing for centuries. In spring these speckled beauties race up the river to spawn. Once they have accomplished that act, if still alive, they find their way back to the sea. There is a certain surety about the process, and Mother Nature administers the process.

In the real world of the modern family, surety—insurance against acts of violence, unrest, or death—is provided through the auspices of a life insurance or casualty insurance company. In rare cases Uncle Sam acts as the insurer of risk. However, in the vast majority of claims in the world of modern capitalism, if a loss is possible, an insurance company, for payment of an insurance premium, will act for people much as Mother Nature acts for the Atlantic salmon.

Gusto is a word not often used when life or casualty insurance is the subject matter. Thus the title of this chapter may come as a jolt to readers who have long been insured under life insurance contracts that they have thought of as anything but tax shelters. This book is about families of mutual funds in their several manifestations, but a little bit of insurance history will help our perspective of how mutual funds fit in with life insurance.

Mutual funds are relative newcomers compared with the life insurance industry. A significant number of the U. S. life insurance companies active today are over 100 years old. American insurance operations were preceded by a few centuries both in England and elsewhere.

Early life insuring operations were *term* in nature, and short term at that. Contracts ran for defined lengths of time, chosen to correspond with real-life events such as the probable duration of voyages. The technical tools of the insurance trade at the time were quite imprecise, with the underlying death rates calculated from data taken from tombstones and church records. Compare these chancy beginnings with the relatively sophisticated start of mutual funds, constructed as they were to deal in the established stock and bond markets at hand in the 1920s.

When the span of insurance was extended from weeks to years, and in due course to the indeterminate remainder of the life insured, the product was perceived to be—with a good deal of help from the sales forces of the companies—a method of substituting a measure of certainty for the substantial uncertainties which have always clouded family lives.

The potential importance of life insurance in family finances was recognized early on, and the role of the state in safeguarding its citizens' rights in the life insurance contract was established more than a century ago. Today life insurance in its non-variable forms remains one of the largest industries regulated primarily by the states. Even in the forms which interest us in this book—variable life and universal variable life—the state regulatory influence continues to be strong.

In their early days, some of the life companies used agency distribution systems that are reasonably close to those which they employ today. (If it ain't broke, don't fix it!) Others shaped their distribution systems to the facts of the times, and the 1890s saw the startling growth of the debit life companies, which matched their agents' practices to the needs of America's urban population at the time. Some of those companies (Metropolitan, Prudential, John Hancock) extended their home-service concept out of the larger cities and became the giants of the business.

INNOVATIONS IN THE LIFE
INSURANCE BUSINESS

Product innovation, which has driven so many other businesses, played little part in the growth pattern of the American life insurance business for a long time. The fundamentals of the business were set very early in the game, and only a finite number of permutations and combinations were possible. Mortality, interest, persistency, taxes, commissions, and expenses were the constituent parts. The business had a heavy regulatory overlay, by the federal government and was regulated by the several states. The valuation and non-forfeiture requirements further limited the ability of the imaginative to produce significant product innovation.

To be sure, there were products generated that were unlike their predecessors. The family income and family maintenance riders were simple tools to facilitate simple estate planning. The guaranteed insurability option cemented down the ability of the insured to obtain additional insurance in the delimited future. The family policy and family rider used aggregates and averages to minimize the number of contracts outstanding, and to steer the family to the appropriate allocation of its premium dollar. But these were relatively simple new insurance products or policy options compared to those which have accompanied the advent of these complex new variable contracts.

ENTER: THE COMPUTER

Mechanization, soon to become full-fledged computerization, had a real impact in controlling the costs of writing and maintaining life insurance contracts. The insurance industry was a computer salesman's fondest dream: huge numbers of similar records, updated regularly through periodic premium payments; massaged this way for billing, that way for commissions, the other way for policy changes, and yet another way for valuation. Economies of scale in the processing areas could be obtained more easily than in other parts of the business, and the increased efficiencies brought by computers effectively neutered the secular rise in costs over several decades.

Computers brought with them a greatly increased ability to do things which simply would not have been attempted a few years earlier. At one time the actuarial literature contained articles dealing with methods of approximating useful functions. Their passing speaks eloquently to the increased capability of computers to simply attack the problem en masse, crunching away at the real numbers until the "right" answer is wrestled to the ground via brute force.

In particular, computers found powerful application in the planning areas, where "what if" games are played in earnest. The ability to whip through the calculations again after slightly changing one of the many inputs proved useful in the extreme. The computer improved the quality of the answers and widened the range of the questions to be asked; but until the advent of the variable era, it, too, did not power product innovation.

In the long decades of largely secular change from 1920 to 1970, the investment departments gradually expanded the areas in which they had an interest, and subsequently the areas in which they had a capability. Without the necessity of a product change in which the policyholder had direct interest in the underlying investments, the investment departments sought diversification strength and enhanced yield in such areas as mortgages, real estate, and common stock. In due course came puts, calls, futures, and options. Here, too, there was innovation in the ways that the reserves for existing products were funded, but no breakthrough in the product area. But the investment officers would be more ready when the variable product time was right.

The marketing and sales areas are where one always finds the greatest innovations. The era preceding the advent of variable products saw substantial experimentation with methods of distribution, in addition to the career life agent and the independent broker.

There was an extended effort to utilize the existing property and casualty (P&C) as a producer of life insurance, with very mixed results. Some outstanding successes (State Farm, Allstate, and Nationwide, for example) sprang from the controlled agent side, but experiments with the truly independent P&C agent were, in general, far less fruitful. This thrust did not hinge on any new product, but was designed to take advantage of the greater frequency of contact the buyer has with the P&C salesperson, and the consequent build-up of trust in that proven supplier.

Innovation has been sought in distribution via sales forces superficially similar to P&C agents—for example, real estate agents. Here the attraction for the carrier is the timely presence on the scene of the real estate broker, privy to the pending sale and in a preferred position for life (at least for mortgage protection) as well as homeowner's and auto coverages. Most of these attempts have not been very productive because of the salespersons' focus on the much larger commission on the sale of the home.

Sometimes the innovative thrust for sales has co-opted erstwhile competitors, as when life insurers seek to market their products through arrangements with banks and savings institutions. The former seek to get closer to where the act of saving is performed; the latter hope to broaden their merchandise line and thereby hold their customer base. There are clear conflicts in the concept as expressed here, but it has worked in practice where the partners have thought deeply about each of their businesses in a customer-centered manner.

The last important way in which distribution innovation has been essayed has been to do it directly from insurer to buyer. The principles of direct-response marketing for a wide range of products are reasonably well known; the challenge has been to make an intangible financial service (which life insurance is) fit within the boundary lines. Examples of success in this undertaking—National Liberty, Colonial Penn, USAA, and The Signature Group—come to mind. Insomniacs among us have watched the emphasis in these marketing efforts shift from direct mail, to media and space advertising, to late-night television and long bouts on drive-time radio.

In sum, progress in the life business has been measured and steady, representing secular improvements in the state of the art. Innovation in the distribution area seems strongest, and has come about by enlisting other possible distribution forces under the life insurance banner. (Changes in the relationship between the individual company and its sales force, such as the rise of the "Personal Producing General Agent," represent a different kind of innovation, one which did not increase the overall sales muscle of the life insurance industry.)

WHAT WERE INSURANCE COMPANIES WAITING FOR?

In looking backwards, a real danger is to ascribe to the players of the time greater foresight than it was possible for them to possess. Yet life insurers (by no means a united group) are always seeking new markets, and they collectively spend a fair piece of change to monitor current developments in prospects' thinking. Further, as do all good businessmen, they watch what and how the competitors are doing. When an opportunity presents itself to diversify profitably and to redeploy their human and fiscal assets to advantage, they seek to move.

ENTER STOCKS AND MUTUAL FUNDS

During this era of down-time in life insurance product innovation, the revolution in mutual funds was indeed beginning. Mutual funds were not without the problems of rising and declining stock markets, nor could the mutual funds match the pocketbooks of the huge mutual life insurers.

However, a growing army of American families were learning to use these new tools as a proxy for building values in savings accounts and life insurance policies. The mutual fund industry had brushed against $50 billion in assets during the 1960s—a tidy sum, and a sum noticed in the board rooms of the powerful life insurance industry.

Early attempts to tie mutual funds to life insurance protection were limited primarily to very small, innovative companies. Western Reserve Life, with Boston's Pioneer Funds, offered single-check programs through which both life insurance for protection and common stock funds for capital growth were purchased. Other small insurers such as Keystone Provident Life and Ozark Life copied this approach using sales phrases such as "Fundowment" and "The Balanced Program" to describe the approach to the salesperson and ultimate consumer.

And, for those with long or bitter memories, there was equity funding. The idea here was to use the values in the policy to purchase the mutual funds, and then use the accumulated value of the funds to pay subsequent insurance premiums. A critical assumption in this approach was that the market would continue to rise apace. After all, looking back at the Dow Jones Industrial Averages for the prior decade, the market looked like a one way street: up!

However, bear markets—such as the crushing events in 1973–74—were indeed in the cards. Worse, the innovator of the idea, Equity Funding Corporation, a growth stock darling of the period, was headed toward extinction. Riddled with fraud, the company went away, and key officers went to the court room.

The equity funding concept did not go away entirely. The sales labels were changed. The buying public has a very short memory for bad news; 3.2 years is the estimate provided by one major graduate school of psychology. Thus insurance companies such as Chubb, Integon, and Pacific Standard Life offer equity funding programs today.

The equity funding approach was likely the first giant step in the direction of variable insurance products—products that combine pure insurance protection with the variable investment returns earned by stocks and bonds, and are offered via an official prospectus filed with the Securities & Exchange Commission and state regulators. However, the packaging poses one long-term problem, and one serious defect considering the tax bill passed in 1986:

- Long-term, the market of stocks needs to rise to create more collateral. If the value of fund shares falls below the outstanding loan, the life insurance policy can be lapsed and the shares sold to pay down the loan balance due. This is bad news for the insured party and the family counting on those assets and the insurance proceeds at death.
- The new tax bill restricts the amount of interest paid that can be used on form 1040 to reduce taxes due. Interest paid on an equity funding type of life insurance policy load will not qualify for full deduction.

The late 1960s was also the time in history for another attempt to combine the virtues of investments with the guarantees of insurance. Thus the investment annuity was developed. The idea was that the insurance company would issue the annuity policy but not deal with the investment of the asset placed in that policy. The insured party could select any type of investment for the annuity, and mutual funds were largely the tools selected.

The investment annuity was primarily a tax-shelter device. Dividend and interest income, and realized capital gains were not subject to tax at either the federal or state level. For that reason, forces in Washington moved swiftly to eliminate the investment annuity. A point to remember, since variable life insurance policies offer the same tax-shelter attributes, is that when Uncle Sam turned off the investment annuity, he grandfathered in the tax preferences for existing policies. Many of these are still in force, and the owners have earned significant investment returns. However, as with the single-check approach—the balanced program—the insurers in this case were small, not the huge eastern mutuals or household names of life insurance.

THE BIG BOYS WERE NOT ASLEEP!

Life insurers acquired more familiarity with the equity part of the securities market as they acquired the power to market and manage separate investment accounts for pension plans, accounts often invested heavily in common stocks. This increased familiarity with direct stock management was limited in practice to the larger companies, but the increased activity was clear to all.

The trend to larger dollar volumes of stock investments in pension plans was much discussed, and life insurers who had found themselves at a disadvantage relative to trust departments had the balance redressed with the creation of the separate account referred to above. Life insurers' pension plans for their own employees came to be substantially equity-based, and the performance of those funds built the conviction that long-term investors in the equity markets of America would do "better." In addition, scholarly discussions regarding the performance of common stocks and stock-based mutual funds relative to bonds showed repeatedly that equities were superior for the long-haul investor. The conclusion was an important one, and theoretically was not confined to pension investors, but to all serious long term investors the modern family planning for retirement or education, and the IRA buyer, for example.

ENTER THE REGISTERED REP

A sales distribution force that we summarily skipped over above is that composed of registered representatives of the Wall Street and financial-planning community. These folks had been used, albeit sparingly, during the years of early innovation—equity funding, the balanced program, and the investment annuity discussed earlier. After all, these products required that the salesperson be licensed to offer both insurance products and investment products. At the time of innovation, very few large Wall Street wirehouses were licensing stock brokers to sell insurance, and the major insurers were just beginning to see merit in selling investments.

Stock brokers had long been regarded by the life insurance sales fraternity as the most vigorous competitors for the serious investment money held by their prospects. The registered representative or financial planner was the access point for the buying public to the great markets in individual stocks and, of late, mutual funds. Three insights prompted more serious consideration of the registered representative (RR) as a distribution channel for some kind of life insurance or annuity product:

1. The productivity of the RR, properly supervised and motivated, was observed to be strong. And much of the product line being sold was similar to insurance merchandise—conservative bonds and bond funds, for example.
2. Arrangements were made between brokerage houses and life insurers for RRs to sell annuities, a moribund and unexciting line for the insurers.
3. Insurers learned first-hand the blandishments of equity sales when some overcame their paranoia about products "not manufactured here," and fear of organized broker-dealers who in turn contracted with outside mutual fund

groups. The Keystone Funds and Massachusetts Financial Services were mutual funds which capitalized early on this new marketing force.

With some sales creativity applied to redesign the product, but no fundamentally different resulting product, the RRs proceeded to tap their market of investors in a very big way. The appeal was different—buyers heard very little about "the income you cannot outlive," but a great deal about "tax-deferred interest build-up." The by-product became the product. The emphasis shifted away from the annuity guarantees, and the RRs were placed on the map as powerful insurance distributors.

The life salesmen registered with these in-house securities departments slowly came to understand the application of mutual funds in the insurance and financial planning situtation. However, they rapidly grasped the notion that the public was interested. In the process there grew a greater appreciation for the salespower which the RR community could mount in selling equities such as mutual funds.

THE NOSE OF THE CAMEL

The selling power of the registered representative; the demonstrated public appetite for indivdual securities, and particularly for the bundled variety (mutual funds); and the continuing unique advantages of conventional life and annuity products all spelled C-A-M-E-L in dozens of planning offices of life insurers and securities firms across the United States. The nose of the beast was the individual variable annuity, which made its debut in the early 1970s.

The individual variable annuity got its design thrust from the greater use in formal employer-employee pension plans of equity investments. "An attempt to put a Maserati engine under the hood of an Edsel" is the way one wag characterized early attempts to meld the existing free-standing equity products with the annuities then funded by the general acount of the life insurer.

A second thrust was to make a vehicle that offered significant tax advantages to the purchaser, as the annuity had always done. Only this time the tax-deferred benefits were not low-octane interest accumulations, but potentially much more high-powered capital gains and dividend accretions flowing from the invested equity base.

The third design consideration was to preserve, and to present to the purchaser of this new hybrid, the advantages of the annuitization principle. Whether the contract was being used to accumulate funds for retirement from periodic deposits, or being used to take a large single deposit to provide for subsequent retirement, the contract contained the resuscitated promise that the retirement payments would last as long as the annuitant. And, the selling story went, unlike the earlier fixed-dollar-funded variety of annuity, the investment in equities would give the hybrid annuity a fighting chance to keep up with inflation.

Viewed from today, the product does not seem startling, but it was quintessential innovation. Those who sought to provide such a desirable product had to find their way through the twin minefields of state regulation of life insurance and federal regulation of the securities business. It is not the purpose of this book to detail the regulatory battles and their resolutions; suffice it to say that in all instances where the two regulatory grids interlock, the resolution sought by pioneers will be long in coming and expensive to come by.

The nose of the camel had entered the tent when the first variable annuity was cleared for sale. Critical questions of regulatory priority, periodic reporting and to whom, appropriate licensing for the carrier and its sales representatives, tax questions, and myriad other items were resolved in the first cut sense.

THE FIRST HUMP

The carriers had been seeking to make their life contracts more flexible and useful to purchasers. Early initiatives went along several routes. Interest-sensitive products freed the buyer from the rigid cage of a lifetime interest assumption by the insurer at the time of policy issue, even allowing for interest adjustments on policies that credited dividends.

Universal life insurance contracts bent the bars of the cage even more. The changed formal structure of the life contract shifted from one in which the face amounts, premiums, and cash values were inextricably tied together into one in which the varying relationships were defined but great flexibilities given to the policyholder. Variable (scheduled premium) life contracts preserved the more traditional structure of the contract, but installed an investment engine other than that of the insurer's general account.

It is worth repeating that the authors give a higher value to those innovations that provoke and require answers to questions not previously asked. Once again the regulatory battles were fought, and in due course the products emerged. Beyond that, much ingenuity and serious money was spent on the new processing systems required for the administration of these more flexible contracts. And basic questions had to be resolved regarding the different licensing and training required by agents to deal effectively with these new creations.

THE REST (AND BEST) OF THE BEAST

Once these products had cleared the mazes and were offered in the marketplace, it was natural evolution for buyers to ask about, sales people to relay opinions upon, and insurers to try to respond to "universal variable life." This product has all the bells and whistles of its predecessors, conveys to the buyer great flexibility at the assumption of some risk, offers a choice of powerplants of varying horsepower, and preserves the traditional tax advantages of life insurance. Furthermore, it preserves those tax advantages in a tax-reform atmosphere that has materially unleveled the playing field for many of the competitors of life insurance. It has come to us through a complex maze of issues that are not entirely resolved, and is powerful stuff when Figure 8–1 is reviewed.

LOOKING THINGS OVER

Let us look at the characteristics of variable universal life, the product that some have dubbed "The Everyman Tax Shelter." Tax shelters are like bomb shelters - what you see is by no means

FIGURE 8–1
WRL Chart (Variable Universal Life and the Advantage of Tax Deferred Growth)

Aside from providing valuable life insurance protection, VUL offers *mutual fund investing* with *tax deferred growth*. Unlike mutual funds not under the tax advantaged umbrella of Variable Universal Life the Tax Reform Act of 1986 did not effect the taxation of funds maintained under VUL products.

The Tax Reform Act did however eliminate the favorable capital gains taxation and dividend exclusion allowance formerly enjoyed by mutual funds outside the VUL product. Accordingly, all dividends and capital gain distributions will be taxed as ordinary income in the year they are apportioned.

Below is an illustrative history of a growth mutual fund with annual investments of $2,000, covering a 30 year period. Over this period of time total dividends of $139,491 and capital gains of $150,823 were apportioned and reinvested in the program. The column at the far right represents a hypothetical 12% yield which approximates the 30 year results of the growth fund.

| | | | Cost of Shares | | | | | Value of Shares | | | | |
Date	Cum. Net Investment	Annual Income Divids	Cum. Income Divids	Total Investment Cost	Annual Cap. Gain Distrib	From Invest.	From Cap. Gain Reinvest.	Sub-total	From Divids Reinvest.	Total Value	12% Interest Projection
12/31/56	2000	67	67	2067	45	1934	45	1979	64	2043	2240
12/31/57	4000	133	200	4200	90	3237	126	3363	170	3533	4749
12/31/58	6000	215	414	6414	154	6802	328	7130	471	7601	7559
12/31/59	8000	280	695	8695	212	9393	573	9966	800	10765	10706
12/31/60	10000	359	1054	11054	290	10870	856	11726	1135	12861	14230
12/31/61	12000	450	1503	13503	837	14803	1814	16617	1763	18380	18178
12/31/62	14000	573	2076	16076	805	14367	2381	16748	2081	18829	22599
12/31/63	16000	727	2803	18803	807	17415	3371	20786	2915	23701	27551
12/31/64	18000	809	3612	21612	1184	20628	4798	25426	3935	29360	33097
12/31/65	20000	924	4535	24535	1608	26210	7247	33457	5569	39027	39309
12/31/66	22000	1074	5609	27609	2167	24560	8561	33121	5878	38999	46266
12/31/67	24000	1268	6877	30877	2266	34067	13404	47471	8890	56361	54058
12/31/68	26000	1628	8506	34506	3642	43145	19696	62841	12301	75142	62785
12/31/69	28000	1822	10328	38328	3178	35316	18291	53607	11331	64938	72559

Date										
12/31/70	30000	2216	12544	42544	4322	33966	20902	54868	12626	67493	83507
12/31/71	32000	2433	14977	46977	1681	38578	24170	62747	15943	78691	95767
12/31/72	34000	2737	17714	51714	3563	43494	29641	73135	19794	92929	109499
12/31/73	36000	3020	20734	56734	4418	40433	30712	71145	20560	91706	124879
12/31/74	38000	3442	24176	62176	4734	31453	26402	57854	18234	76088	142105
12/31/75	40000	4143	28319	68319	1465	43818	36443	80262	28082	108344	161397
12/31/76	42000	4656	32976	74976	2168	59403	49886	109289	41601	150890	183005
12/31/77	44000	5575	38550	82550	4733	59348	53088	112436	45972	158408	207206
12/31/78	46000	6429	44979	90979	5474	63893	61526	125420	54690	180110	234310
12/31/79	48000	7747	52726	100726	5960	78530	80367	158897	73891	232788	264668
12/31/80	50000	9937	62663	112663	8321	97896	107581	205477	101248	306725	298668
12/31/81	52000	12991	75654	127654	9138	89243	104978	194221	103145	297367	336748
12/31/82	54000	14563	90217	144217	18570	92439	128231	220670	121341	342011	379398
12/31/83	56000	15022	105238	161238	17305	108098	166509	274606	154749	429355	427166
12/31/84	58000	16420	121659	179659	19437	100089	169871	269959	157662	427621	480665
12/31/85	60000	17832	139491	199491	22249	117549	222037	339586	201821	541406	540585
Cumulative Totals		$139,491	$139,491		$150,823						

Assumptions: 28% Tax Bracket
Dividends   = $139,491
Capital Gains   =   150,823
Taxable Income = $290,314

Assuming a continuous 28% tax bracket over the 30 year period, $81,287 in taxes have been payable, which computes to average yearly taxes of $2,709 over the lifetime of the investment if the average tax savings of $2,709 were redirected into a tax deferred growth account earning 12%, an ADDITIONAL $732,222 DOLLARS would accumulate.

what you get. In some cases the difference is positive—the shelter may be aesthetically pleasing, or useful in peacetime as a root cellar. In other instances negatives may appear—the salesman did not say that they are dank, dark, claustrophobic, and that you may be required to let the neighbors in if Murphy's Law plays a dirty trick.

The Upside

1. Variable universal life is, indeed, a life insurance policy and carries a death benefit from the moment of policy issue.

This point is all too often lost in the characterization of the variable insurance product as a tax shelter. While we do not (or do not like to) think of these policies in this way, there is a significant gain over "investment" to the beneficiary in the event of an early death by the insured. So aside from a variety of other pluses, the death benefit in the policy is present and can be a significant positive.

2. Investment earnings within the life insurance contract accumulate on a tax-deferred basis.

This is the characteristic termed "inside build-up" by insurance professionals. It is true of all ordinary or whole life contracts, those policies that have a cash value buildup. In the case of variable life/variable universal life (VL/VUL) contracts, the investment earnings can be interest, dividends, or capital gains. The difference between taxable and tax-free accumulations is clearly shown in Figure 8–1

3. If the contract is in force when the insured person dies, the VL/VUL policy will have provided not merely tax deferral, but tax avoidance.

Under these circumstances—death of the insured party and payment of policy benefits to the named beneficiary—the build-up of sheltered assets in the policy *is never taxable*. Thus cradle-to-grave tax freedom is possible, at least under present tax rules. In Figure 8–2 the compounding power is illustrated over a 60-year period.

> **4.** The VL/VUL contract typically provides an attractive array of investment alternatives within the life insurance policy.

Money deposited can be initially positioned in one or several of these alternatives, which normally will include a cash-type fund, bond fund, blue chip stock, and growth fund. Thus the owner of the policy can match the desired asset allocation model or risk tolerance as discussed in earlier chapters. The "Rule of 6" might be useful for this exercise.

> **5.** The insurance contract gives the owner the privilege of switching between the internal funds (reallocating the initial investment choices). The owner can do so at zero or minimal cost for a reasonable number of transfers.

Thus the owner determines the timing of investment selection and reallocation of assets at low or no cost. Two of the most important words in investing, we are reminded, are "liquidity" and "flexibility." The VL/VULs handle both of those neatly.

> **6.** Because the contract is a life policy, such transfers take place within in it, and have no present tax consequence.

Thus, unlike taxable mutual funds held personally by a taxpayer, adjustments of risk level or reallocation of assets in these variable policies are not a tax events. The insurance company does not send a dreaded form 1099 detailing taxable transactions from the prior year.

> **7.** The contract may be borrowed against under quite liberal conditions.

The net cost of borrowing typically runs between 0.75 percent and 2.00 percent. There are no tax consequences to borrow-

FIGURE 8–2
Illustration of Variable Life Insurance

Male Issue Age 35   Annual Premium for Preferred Class: $1,320
                           $100,000 Policy Specified Amount
                           Option B Death Benefit
                           Assumed Hypothetical Gross
                           Annual Investment Rate of Return: 12%

End of Policy Year	Premiums Accumulated at 5%	Cash Value[1,2]	Death Benefit[1,2]
1	1,386	408	100,408
2	2,841	1,515	101,515
3	4,369	2,722	102,722
4	5,974	4,038	104,038
5	7,659	5,473	105,473
6	9,427	7,037	107,037
7	11,285	8,740	108,740
8	13,235	10,597	110,597
9	15,283	12,629	112,629
10	17,433	14,841	114,841
11	19,691	17,264	117,264
12	22,061	19,907	119,907
13	24,550	22,791	122,791
14	27,164	25,941	125,941
15	29,908	29,360	129,360
16	32,789	33,085	133,085
17	35,815	37,137	137,137
18	38,991	41,560	141,560
19	42,327	46,380	146,380
20	45,829	51,649	151,649
25	66,150	86,061	186,061
30	92,084	138,856	238,856
35	125,184	220,785	320,785
40	167,428	348,406	448,406
45	221,344	546,336	646,336
50	290,156	853,976	953,976
55	377,979	1,333,948	1,433,948
60	490,066	2,093,612	2,193,612

[1]Assumes a $1,320 premium is paid at the beginning of each Policy year. Values would be different if Premiums are paid with a different frequency or in different amounts. [2]Assumes current cost of insurance charges have been imposed.

Source: Western Reserve Life Assurance Co. of Ohio. Used with permission.

ing cash values under the conditions defined by the policy. However, as noted elsewhere in this chapter, the interest paid on policy loans will not be fully tax-deductible.

8. Because the contract is universal in nature, there is no obligation to pay premiums regularly.

Policy lapse is not triggered by failure to adhere to a premium payment schedule, as is the case with conventional term and ordinary life insurance. Rather, the assets held in the policy—the cash or investment values—are used to offset premiums and other charges currently due.

9. Because the VUL is funded by separate accounts of the insurer, the policy funding—the owner's investment account—is independent of the solvency of the life insurer.

In recent years the insurance industry has experienced some woes. Two major issuers of annuities were on the brink of collapse. Other insurers own huge amounts of junk bonds that are clearly speculative in nature. Thus having the policy values held in a separate account is a valuable plus.

10. The majority of policy designs call for the premium payments to be fully invested immediately, with the acquisition costs recouped via surrender charges.

Serious long-term purchasers can escape the impact of overt sales charges entirely. Therefore, the VL/VUL policies, with some exceptions, can be no-load in nature for long-term holders. The holding period required to escape all charges varies. However, five to ten years is the industry range at this time for policies the authors have reviewed.

The Downside

1. Buyers whose self-image is that of an investor need to grasp that they are indeed buying a life insurance policy.

This means they are paying for life insurance protection itself, and while the benefits can be assigned value as part of the package, there is little intrinsic value if the buyer does not need more coverage. The majority of charges in the expense matrix relate to the operation and administration of a life contract. In the aggregate, such charges can exert significant drag on the possible investment performance of the program. Thus finding the best family of variable product clones is a critical decision if earnings are to offset all internal costs and still produce generous returns.

    2. While the investment earnings do accumulate within the policy in a tax-deferred manner, the buyer should understand that "tax-deferred" is not the same as "tax-free."

Should the variable policy ever be surrendered, for example, the owner is then liable for tax on the excess of the cash value accumulation over the original investment in the contract. Given the accumulation power of the more aggressive equity vehicles, this tax liability could prove to be a nasty surprise some day. But it bears pointing out again that should death occur while the insurance policy is in force, the investment account within the contract will have accomplished tax avoidance, not merely tax deferral.

    3. The flexibility to initially position money in several alternatives, and to reposition it at discretionary intervals, brings with it the necessity for the buyer to shoulder the responsibility for periodically rethinking the asset allocation and risk situtaion.

The onus is clearly on the owner of the policy and no longer on the life insurance company, which presumably has considerable depth and knowledge in the investment area. Strategies such as the "D" series can be useful. Market timing and the "Rule of 6" can be helpful. Willy-nilly trading of assets in the policy simply because it is cheap, and no immediate tax event is triggered, should be discouraged. After all, these are life insurance contracts and should be considered serious long-term investments.

4. Thoughtful switching can enhance the value of the account materially; however, ability to switch carries with it the downside possibility of poor timing in the process, with the consequence of results worse than buy-and-hold.

A very important caution indeed. After all, the assets are compounding on a tax-deferred (potentially tax-free) basis. Thus, without taxation and good manager selection, the results should be upscale. Market timing these assets, while attractive on paper or in retrospect, could prove foolhardy.

5. It is easy to overlook the necessity for the insurer to repay itself for outstanding policy loans from the policy proceeds in a death claim.

Using the variable policy for borrowing could leave the beneficiaries with a lot less than all parties had figured on. The life insurance company is going to pay itself back first, and send the beneficiaries a less-full bag!

6. Most sophisticated purchasers find the notion of life insurance premium payments as "forced savings" to be amusing at the least, and as applicable to "the other guy" at most.

The absence of the forcing device in the variable product may account for badly underfunded policies (and underfulfilled plans) for both the novice and the sophisticate alike. VL/VULs are serious long-term financial and estate planning tools and should be dealt with as such.

In the next chapter we will look at what variations exist among variable products, and what guideposts can be established for choosing the insurer and policy type that fit your individual circumstances. Each policy is a little different. Numerous factors beyond selection of the asset manager must be dealt with to connect with the variation that you, the insured, can live with for the long term.

The process of selection should be no more difficult than finding the correct fly in the cluttered fly box, or the correct water to cast to. Indeed, fishing for the right answers to the key questions could be worth a bundle some day.

CHAPTER 9

FINANCIAL PLANNING ASPECTS OF VARIABLE UNIVERSAL LIFE

"Unquestionably, there is progress. The average American now pays out almost as much in taxes alone as he formerly got in wages."

H. L. Mencken, 1949

We have seen how products in both industries—regular mutual funds and variable insurance products—have developed separately. More recently, they have begun to come together, and one result is variable universal life. Clearly that product will have many uses in financial planning, estate planning, and general tax thinking as the present decade winds down and we move into the 1990s.

Let's consider some uses of the product in reducing federal and state income taxes. It would be hard to overstate the aversion which many people have to paying taxes. One of the miracles of the American economy is the very high percentage of compliance with the tax laws in the face of that distaste. The variable universal life contract offers the tax-averse taxpayer a thoughtful tool. A feel for the tax question was developed in Chapter 7.

TAX SAVINGS

An Alternative to the Savings Account

Probably the most common "investments" by Americans are life insurance policies and savings accounts. To the realm of savings accounts we can add checking accounts that earn interest, and shares in a credit union and savings & loan. These savings accounts hold billions of family dollars, the bulk of which stayed there through the era of high returns on short-term money. Why? Because the American saver sought a "safety net" and a perceived "reasonable" return. As noted in Chapter 4, the actual returns earned by these folks, net of taxes and inflation, were small indeed.

The money that left those savings accounts did so because some savers did not find the returns at the savings bank to be reasonable. That money today is largely in money market funds, or has come back into the banking system in money market accounts. The yield difference is not significant.

The situation for savers today is that savings yields in such accounts are low, *and they are taxable.* One of the investment choices in a universal variable insurance policy often is a money market account. Inside the policy, however, the interest is not currently taxable. The buyer of the policy can match (or better) the interest return and have it on a tax-deferred basis to boot!

While not quite as convenient as the savings account, the owner can get the money available in the policy quickly enough for practical purposes. And a great deal of the money in savings accounts is serious savings, not subject to short-term withdrawals. For many of these savers, variable universal life (or in this case, just universal life) offers an alternative with a tax advantage.

An Alternative for the Conservative Investor

Many savers want to invest their money directly, not bank it, in a conservative way. These savers have bought bonds outright, or have chosen to purchase mutual bond funds. They want a higher yield and have accepted some risk to their principal in return. Some of these bond investors have bought low-risk government bonds, others have purchased corporate bonds or bond funds, and others the junk bonds that have been discussed in prior chapters. These bond funds share one thing in common: their interest is taxable by both Uncle Sam and a growing number of states.

Variable universal life policies commonly contain an investment choice of a high-quality bond fund. That bond fund can accommodate conservative investors with a similar vehicle in terms of market risk. The important difference is that the interest credited is not currently taxable inside the variable universal life policy. Over a long span, the serious investor will see a major difference in the compounding power of money accumulated on a tax-deferred versus a taxable basis.

Mention should be made of the several funds of zero coupon securities that are included in the fund families inside some commercially available VULs. Introduced into the marketing equation at a time when interest rates were very high, these "funds of zeros" were the principal power plants for earlier versions of the contract. Available in free-standing form, such funds have the undesireable characteristic of generating annual tax liabilities, but paying no coupons to the buyer from which she or he can pay the taxes. Inside the VUL, the cloned "zero funds" shed that negative aspect, since the tax-deferral nature of the contract defers even these taxes.

An Alternative for the Buy-and-Hold Equities Investor

Many investors in the stock market buy and hold individual stock and bond issues. The stock is often sold when some life event requires funds, not always to purchase another security. This kind of investor does not actively trade investment positions, such as stocks owned, but prefers to have the funds "in the market."

Two of the investment options common to universal variable life policies are the quality stock fund, and the more aggressive growth stock fund. These provide alternatives for buy-and-hold investors, and offer varying degrees of risk and reward. In addition, these stock market alternatives offer continuous investment management without sentimental attachment. These managers are free to sell the shares on investment merit, a possible plus for the buy-and-hold stock market investor.

A third option is becoming available to investors in newer versions of the VUL. Opportunities to invest in real estate are being offered in certain products. It affords the chance to participate in this large investment sector, and to do so in a way that is less illiquid and more flexible than direct investment.

Capital gains now are taxed on the same basis as dividends and interest. Therefore the same advantage of tax-deferred income (in this case, short-term and long-term capital gains) is true. The buyer of the variable universal life contract has this advantage, where the owner of conventional taxable mutual funds does not.

An Alternative for the Timer and Trader

Certain investors like to manage their holdings actively, either by themselves or with their broker. Many such investors have turned to families of funds because of the ease of trading between funds in the family. A consideration for traders or timers using either stocks or funds is the capital gains tax incurred when one security is sold and another bought. A further factor is the cost of commissions in individual stock trading. These issues—active asset allocation and market timing—were dealt with at length in Chapters 3 through 5. With the personal computer becoming a usable reality for millions of families, we would suggest that the use of active trading programs utilizing mutual fund-type investments will increase quite a lot in years to come.

The variable universal life policy eliminates the commission factor just as did the family of freestanding funds. The policy permits a generous number of free switches in the course of a year. Additional switches are at modest cost. And the tax bogey is removed, since the changes are tax-deferred: Uncle Sam does not keep score of these transactions. Thus VUL affords a family of mutual funds, and the timing/trading investor should make sure the family has the appropriate variety of investment vehicles for the trading activity desired.

FLEXIBILITY

Much has been written about the tax-saving aspect of variable life insurance. The actual insurance policy possesses unusual flexibility as well, which is helpful in estate and financial planning.

Funding Flexibility

Financial or estate planning is a continuous process. Once a plan is put in place to fit the original circumstances, it must be regularly monitored. People's life situations change enough over the short term to warrant plan changes. This is true in wills, in investments such as mutual funds, and in life insurance as well.

The variable universal life contract has set the family of funds inside the life insurance contract. This puts the investment flexibility inside as well. Quite aside from the positive tax consequences discussed above, this arrangement helps the planner cope with change.

It is common to find this kind of pattern in investment thinking over a lifetime. Young singles can have meaningful discretionary income so that—after appropriate liquid savings—investment for growth is possible. If they become young marrieds, the possibilities for investment may be accentuated. It depends on the tug between couple-oriented spending and goal-oriented savings. Should they begin a family and/or buy a house, the time focus shifts toward the present for most of their money. For education, however, the horizon shifts ahead 18 years or so. When child-rearing is past, attention needs to be paid to funding the enjoyment of the time together. Then comes the focus on planning for retirement. And then the concentration on conservation and liquidation of the retirement funds.

These shifts from aggressive to conservative and back again occur in all lives. They are obscured by a host of short-term factors: the market, current interest rates, current needs and opportunities. But they need to be dealt with to make the best lifetime use of your money. Life-cycle investment decisions have been discussed elsewhere in the book.

We need to emphasize that all the trendlines show that Americans are seeking better personal control over their financial affairs. After a long love affair with fixed-income and low-risk alternatives, people today seem willing to assume more risk to obtain more reward. The traditional places for savings—the savings banks and the life insurers—did not provide that element of personal management. As part of its flexibility, the VUL puts control of the underlying investment choices in the investors' hands. If the program works well, wonderful! If it works out poorly, the investor is the driver—that's the way people are coming to want it. And that's precisely the way the new variable universal life sets it up for the policy owner.

With a family of funds (representing different positions on the capital-market line) inside the life contract, shifts in funding are easily accomplished. Tax matters aren't valued out of proportion, commission costs are zero, and the moves can be done by telephone.

Further, the investments can be in any or all of the investment options, though some minimum account size is usually required. The reward can be tailored to the risk the owner is willing to carry. All of the positioning and repositioning techniques spelled out in Chapters 4 through 6 can be used, right inside the insurance policy!

Life Insurance Flexibility

As a family changes, the insurance itself needs to change. Death benefits required to do the job increase as income rises, family size expands, and inflation presses on the cost of things. Parents need no more illustration of this than the escalating and often prohibitive cost of providing funds for college education!

Not everything rises forever. Life insurance needs can go down as fewer family members are dependent. Life needs can decrease as retirement income builds up in an employer pension plan. How desirable it would be to easily accommodate the expansions and contractions in coverage, without, for example, buying new policies or canceling old ones.

In the same way that needs (and death benefits) change, the ability of the individual or family to pay premiums changes. Advancing up the job ladder brings better pay and stronger savings. Two incomes for a single family may provide an opportunity to put more money away. Conversely, most families experience a layoff or a period between jobs. The necessity to meet regular fixed commitments can really pinch. And most American families put a high value on life insurance premium payments.

Once again variable universal life provides the convenient answer. Death benefits can be decreased at any time and to any amount, subject to policy provisions. The death benefit can also be increased, subject to good health. Premium payments can be increased in good times. They can be cut back or stopped in hard times. Single amounts, such as contest winnings or an inheritance, can be "dropped into" the policy. Wonderful flexibility is available to the buyer and to the planner in a single instrument!

SOME TRANSITIONAL SITUATIONS

During 1987, we made the transition between the old tax act and the new one. Here are some situations in which people disadvantaged by the change, or by current circumstances, can use these new variable universal products positively.

The Holder of Maturing CD's

All kind of investors and savers bought certificates of deposit back when their yields were 16 percent and greater. Even the holders of the longest term certificates can see the approaching date when the certificate proceeds must be reinvested. Looking at the current short-term investment landscape is not heartening. Yields are not within shouting distance of those on maturing certificates. What to do?

Some investors in this situation have been using single premium variable universal life policies to receive the lump-sum proceeds of their certificates. They wish to escape the federal income tax they paid each year on their old certificates. And, having seen the roller-coaster ride that interest rates have taken, they want a choice of investment vehicles to move between. These investors have been splitting their proceeds between several of the investment options available in the policies, maintaining safety in the bond funds and seeking better overall returns in the stock or growth fund alternatives.

The Investor Hurt by 401-K Changes

These investors used to be able to make larger contributions to their 401-K plans. Such contributions were tax-deductible, and the plan then sheltered the accumulations. With reduced contribution limits now in force, these investors are looking at variable insurance contracts to accommodate part of their regular contributions.

While they cannot get present tax deductibility for their contribution, they can put it in a more flexible tax shelter via the VUL. And they can get additional sharply priced life insurance as a convenient part of the process.

THREE SPECIAL SITUATIONS

We have been looking at applications of the variable universal life policy that can apply to many investors. The authors think it is a better way to do things in most cases. The reader will note the continuing positive stress on personal control of the active investment element of the VUL. We consider that a unique and quite useful element in financial planning.

The VUL has special suitability for selected situations. We have chosen to illustrate three. The first, "RICO"—after the Edward G. Robinson movie on organized crime during Prohibition—speaks to protecting the assets of those exposed to the stiff penalties contained in the 1986 federal tax blockbuster. The second, "Malpractice," is relevant to professionals in all areas who have a professional liability exposure, and quite possibly to officers and directors of corporations. The third, "Financial Aid Form," applies to parents of college-bound children.

RICO: A Deadly Game

Can the saver or investor have any fun with these variable insurance contracts, or is the game deadly serious throughout? RICO, and discussions that follow about malpractice and college costs, are the fun parts of this exercise.

RICO is a body of federal legislation designed to deal with organized crime. The term RICO stands for "Racketeer Initiated Criminal Organizations." "What," you ask, "does a criminal organization have to do with a book on the modern mutual fund family and variable insurance products?" Read on! RICO, while meant for the bad guys, may affect many readers and millions of American families.

The bill was enacted to attack organized criminal organizations. In substance, the judicial aspects are built around mail, wire, and securities fraud. Prove two instances of any of these, and the federal court system will cheerfully hear the case.

However, a civil side was written into the bill by Congress. Thus, while not a RICO in a criminal context, anyone accused of multiple mail, securities, or wire fraud can be brought to task under its terms. Thus a scrambled business or family relationship that meets the RICO tests might find its way to federal rather than the state courts. Why?

- RICO offers the winner in court automatic triple damages. In state courts the judge or jury sets the amount of the award, if any.
- State courts are running years behind the growing case load. Thus the case may not be heard for years to come.

These are two very powerful immediate benefits for the folks making the claim. The case will likely be heard far more swiftly if brought under RICO, and the award is a predetermined triple, plus court costs. But what is the relationship between RICO cases and variable insurance products?

1. Assets deposited in the various investment options in the policy are deemed, while so deposited, to be the asset of the life insurance company. Readers will recall that those assets are the source of mortality and other costs collected by the insurer.
2. The protection element of the policy—the actual amount of insurance protection in force—is the property of the named beneficiary at the demise of the insured party.

Thus the policy assets—those investments that we have spoken about at length throughout this and the previous chapter— are not available to the courts to settle judgments. There are wrinkles, such as declaration of bankruptcy, that can flaw these protections. Many states, of course, recognize the creditor-exemption statutes which protect the owner/insured under a broad range of circumstances, and the spendthrift clause which protects the beneficiaries under appropriate conditions. These statutes and clauses provide strong protection when the court speaks.

The number of RICO cases is explosive. A Senate legal advisor told the authors that the case load was rising at 600 percent a year, and that cases were being heard on all manner of complaints—alimony and a variety of securities fraud arguments, for example.

Will the reader be a target in the unfunny world of RICO? One can never be sure. These are litigious times. The world becomes more complex each day. Thus, depositing some important family assets in a variable insurance contract as a first line of defense can be good financial planning.

As with the malpractice discussion to follow, a word of caution vis-à-vis RICO defense measures. It is crucial to determine the status of the state you live in vis-à-vis the treatment of these statutes and clauses. The authors have checked some jurisdictions; Massachusetts, Pennsylvania, and Florida are among those where this protection seems to work.

Malpractice

Who hasn't read the newspapers lately without reading about a malpractice award? In fact, in one recent issue of our local rag six were listed, and the area business magazine ran a special issue on the topic.

The number of malpractice cases is rising fast enough to figuratively bury the court system. The size of court awards—and out of court settlements—is rising even faster. Malpractice insurance premiums are large enough to force practitioners to leave the medical field, or restrict practice to hospitals and other institutions that carry ample coverages. And, in some medical specialties, insurance coverages have been reduced to levels well below typical court awards.

When a malpractice case is resolved in the courtroom, and the claim exceeds the level of the insurance coverage available to the loser—doctor, dentist, or other professional—the court will go after other personally held assets, including IRA, Keogh, or other retirement accounts.

As in the case of RICO, the variable life contract may provide a thick layer of asset protection for saved and invested funds. The doctor, fearful of a malpractice claim—and which doctor isn't?—can park some saved assets in the variable policy and reduce the risk of creditor claims, including those of the courts. Some cautions, however:

- As with RICO, state rules should be checked to determine whether the creditor-exemption statutes and spendthrift clause apply in your jurisdiction.
- Also, purchase of the variable contract should be made prior to notice that a major malpractice is in the offing. If a registered letter of notification of preliminary hearings has been received, it is probably too late to use this wonderful device!
- Lastly, the authors would recommend that the policy values stay put in the policy. If the court sees active borrowing activity by the owner or insured, it may view the whole transaction as a sham, not part of a long-term serious financial planning effort.

With RICO and malpractice we see these variable life products performing on a different stage than we have discussed earlier. To this point, the focus has been on tax advantages, insurance benefits, investment structures, and economies of ownership. Applying the variable policy asset to the practical issue of defending assets from creditor claim magnifies the usefulness of these new products by a mile.

Beyond creditor claim protection lies the largest and most valuable benefit that variable life can bring to the largest number of readers—as a working tool to help in the struggle for survival in the college tuition area.

The Cost of Education

Some 22 million young Americans are teen-agers in the age range thirteen to eighteen. Behind these there is a somewhat larger audience of 28 million pre-teens in the age range eight to twelve. A large number of these would like to attend the college or university of their choice. The parents of these children dream endlessly about attending that college graduation—"my daughter the doctor," and so forth. Figure 9–1 documents the rising costs of tuition on the basis of national averages.

The college of choice these days can be very, very expensive, however desirable. The number of institutions of higher education charging more than $10,000 per year rises with each tuition announcement letter that parents receive. The number whose total costs are approaching $20,000 a year is also clearly on the rise.

Thus a family with three children embarked on the educational highway at many eastern private colleges is looking at a set of staggering tuition bills—in present dollars, at the high-

FIGURE 9–1

U.S. College Costs (Tuition and Fee Costs for Public and Private Colleges and Universities, by Year)

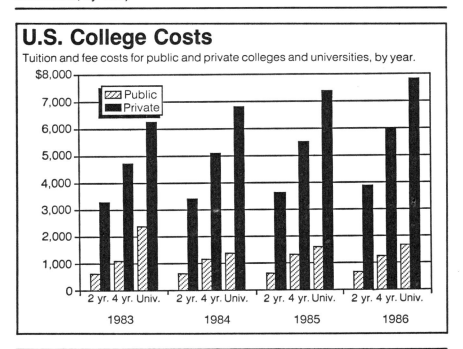

Source: U.S. Department of Education

est-priced institutions, close to $200,000. That cost is rising at between 8 and 10 percent each year.

As with RICO and malpractice, you may want to ask, "What does this have to do with a book on investments, mutual fund families, and variable insurance products?" The answer is: very little if the subject is conventional mutual funds or shares of stock held personally; but quite a lot if the subject shifts to variable insurance policies and the assets held therein.

The Financial Aid Form

As each child intent on entering college sees the vision a year or two away and begins to make inquiries, a form will be made available from the high school's guidance department. This is the Financial Aid Form required by most colleges and universities, and it is a horror to deal with—certainly more so than the filing of your tax return each year!

The FAF, as the form is politely referred to, asks for data on a variety of financial and other subjects. The purpose of the FAF exercise is to determine on a standardized basis how much college cost the family can handle versus how much financial aid the federal and state governments and the university might have to provide. Thus the questions relate closely to those obvious assets that will be available to cover educational costs and housing.

1. How much equity exists in the family home, if any? That, simply stated, is the estimated market value of the home less the amount of the mortgage.

If there is a lot of free value in the home, the college financial aid officers will regard that family as financially stronger and better able to contribute to the costs of attending college. While the family is neither required nor urged to mortgage its home outright, nor to set up an equity line against it, when the family contribution is determined this way there are few alternatives. This is particularly painful if the mortgage balance has been systematically reduced as the children grew up, and inflationary forces in the late 1970s and early 1980s added significantly to real or perceived value.

2. Income of the family and the prospective college student will be reported. This includes earnings from employment or business, and also interest and dividend earnings, such as might come from stock ownership, mutual funds, or savings accounts.

3. Other assets of the family and the student will be inventoried. Some will count in the FAF calculation, some will not. The intelligent self-interest of the family unit is served by considering how its assets are distributed between those that count in the FAF calculation, and those that do not.

The College Scholarship Service, armed with data taken from the FAF, applies the complicated tests and formulae that go into determining the "expected family contribution." They do this for several million families that submit the FAF each year. Families and students applying represent an enormous range of personal financial (and demographic) situations. The complex calculations represent a search for an equitable family contribution from all—an enormously challenging assignment performed by computer.

People have egos. That includes the moms and dads (with misty eyes for the best college education available) of the aspiring high school graduates. Ego can really be a costly enemy in the FAF procedure. "Our house is worth more than that!" "Our business (or securities owned) is worth more too!" Those ego knee-jerks can lift the tuition contribution by a country mile because that dispassionate FAF computer in New Jersey records the higher amounts and judges more assets to be available to the college bursar. The computer has no way of outguessing the numbers presented!

The whole story is a lot more complex than we describe in this chapter. In fact, judging from our experience, a complete and detailed book on this subject, approaching the process entirely from the family's point of view, would be worthwhile reading for millions of Americans faced with the growing tuition-payment dilemma.

But, the bad news behind us, we can move on to the good news that variable life and variable universal life bring to the college-cost clambake.

1. The FAF form does not ask questions about life insurance assets. Thus these do not count when the college aid computer does its evaluation. Such life insurance assets (cash values) can be thought of as "good" ones. Variable universal life shares this attribute with all other forms of life insurance, but has the unique feature that the insured controls the distribution of his or her assets inside the VUL policy. It's clear that the VUL makes it possible to approximate, within the policy, your existing asset holdings outside the policy.

2. Rather than waiting to borrow on the home to pay the tuition, why not borrow before the FAF form is asked for, and use the loan proceeds to retire all other forms of outstanding debt? That approach is likely to cut your cost of borrowing, make your interest costs fully deductible, and reduce the value of your home as that major asset is valued in the FAF calculation. In addition, the flexibility provided by an equity line of credit will give you the assurance of liquidity you need to make the important changes sketched in the next item.

3. Before the FAF is on the kitchen table or your desk, you should consider liquidating free-standing taxable investments and savings, and repositioning these in the variable insurance product of your choosing. Any penalties, commission costs, or tax burden you experience will contrast vividly with your subsequent investment experience under the VUL. The life insurance can be made to insure the income producer(s) who provide the family contribution that makes college feasible. And the beauty part is that those assets and the income and/or capital gains they provide do not count in the calculations made by that busy computer in Princeton.

The VL/VULs have now done something of value that conventional mutual funds simply cannot do. These "uninsured" funds surely would be sold to pay tuition. Quite possibly the assets held in the insurance policy will still be in place on graduation day. Which course and result would you prefer?

Conventional ordinary or whole life insurance has always been available for the FAF purpose, as well as for creditor protection from RICO and malpractice. However, there is a very important distinction to be made where comparing the traditional life insurance vehicles with this new breed of policy.

- In the traditional policies, the policy asset is managed by the life insurance company. We have noted elsewhere in the text that these folks are capable managers of bonds and real estate, but not nearly as capable with blue chip and growth stocks as the great mutual fund groups.
- In the variable insurance product area, you—the owner or insured—control the investment destiny, as noted earlier in this chapter.

Thus the conventional policies of old hold little of the investment attraction of the new breed, and there are limitations on using them in some of the powerful ways we have discussed in this chapter. Many more creative uses will be discovered as variable policies earn their keep.

CHOOSING A POLICY

Even the best plans don't count unless they are implemented. There comes a time to put the ball in play, and the buyer must choose a company to provide the policy. The thrust of this book has been to highlight the investment flexibility of this entire class of policies. In the next chapter we discuss how to use the factors analyzed in the first seven chapters to choose an appropriate family of funds inside the life contract. For many investors, that will be the most important facet of the decision.

But there are features and charges in the life contract itself, called the "wrapper" by some, that are important in determining what the ultimate cost of the product will be. To simplify and focus this discussion, we will direct our attention to the single premium version of the variable universal product (by far the more important one in the marketplace).

AVAILABILITY

As this is written, fewer than 20 companies are approved to issue the most flexible form of this product on the annual-payment basis. Fewer than 30 have approval to do it on a single-premium basis. An additional 10 companies are in registration on each basis. Why is this? Does the buyer have reasonable access to variable universal life?

The costs of getting into the VUL business are very high; thus nearly all companies offering it are large ones. Legal expenses are significant, new handling systems must be built, and agents and brokers need to be trained and registered or licensed. Sales material carefully explaining the characteristics of the product must be drafted. It appears that the majority of life insurers will not enter the business because of heavy costs of design and operation.

Fortunately for the buyer, those companies already in the business have broad sales networks. Most distribute their policies through their own agents, through insurance brokers, and through securities salespeople. (Any salesperson must be both licensed to sell life insurance, and registered to sell mutual funds. In addition, some states require sales agents to pass a specific test on variable products.) The product is heavily advertised, and in the real world you should have no trouble finding a salesperson who can help you.

FEATURES

Death Benefit

The death benefit is generally available in two patterns. The first is like traditional whole life, in which the death benefit generally remains level and includes your fund portfolio value.

This option helps lower your insurance costs because the amount of insurance you pay for is reduced by the fund portfolio value. At longer durations, if the fund should accumulate substantially, the amount of the death benefit will rise.

The second option is an increasing death benefit, representing the insurance amount plus the value of the fund portfolio at the time of death. Additional flexibility is provided by the privilege of changing from one option to the other during the life of the policy.

A feature included in some policies, but not in all, is the minimum death benefit. This provision guarantees that the death benefit will not drop below a specified amount, irrespective of the performance (or lack of it) in the variable life funds' performance.

Optional Riders

For typical policies, riders may be attached to accomplish these things:

- Add additional death benefits on the life of the insured;
- Add death benefits on children (or on spouse and children);
- Guarantee that you can buy additional coverage for a specified time into the future without regard to your health;
- Provide coverage against accidental death;
- Provide that the insurance company will pay the premiums if you are disabled;
- Provide that the insurer will pay you a disability income if you are disabled.

These riders can tailor the basic policy. With all the flexibility the VUL provides, the riders can make it fit your family situation even more closely.

Minimums and Maximums

The minimum policy is set on a premium basis for the single premium policies that have been the most popular type to date. The companies are about equally divided between minimum single premiums of $5,000 and $10,000. We should note that most single premium policies are written so the buyer can make occasional additional deposits to that "single" premium.

For flexible premium contracts (annual pay, or more often) the minimums are set in the conventional way; that is, by face amount. Here the companies are split between $50,000 and $100,000, with a sprinkling at $25,000. In addition, there may be minimum premium payments, such as $600 per year.

Most of us, readers and authors alike, are not affected much by the maximums set by the life insurance companies. For the record, let it be said that most carriers will accept $1,000,000 as a single premium deposit. That amount is influenced by the amount of insurance the single premium will buy, which can be very substantial at younger ages. Here, traditional underwriting considerations come into play.

Special Policyholder Rights

The purchaser of a variable universal life contract has the right conferred on him by the so-called "free look" provision to return the contract to the issuing company within a limited period and get a return payment. The period provided is ten days after it was delivered or 45 days after the contract was applied for. The return payment is commonly the full initial premium payment, although it may be the account value of the initial amount invested less any deductions made therefrom.

There is an exchange provision, running for 18 to 24 months from the date of issue, which permits the owner to exchange the policy for a fixed premium/fixed benefit contract. You must make the request in writing and return the variable policy. The fixed policy will be issued as of the original date, and no evidence of insurability (good health) need be furnished.

Withdrawals and Loans

Once the policy is under way, the owner may make a partial withdrawal from the cash value. Any excess of this withdrawal over the cost basis in the contract (the sum of the premiums paid) is taxable, but in general partial withdrawals can be scheduled so that no tax is incurred.

The owner may also make policy loans subject to the guidelines in the policy. Loans may be restricted in the first year and subject to some percentage in subsequent years. There is a policy-loan interest rate charged, and a separate rate of interest credited to the borrower. The spread between these rates is what counts, since it is your net cost of borrowing from the policy.

On flexible premium contracts, the maximum spread runs from 1.0 percent to 3.5 percent, with an average near 2.5 percent. On single premium contracts, the maximum spread ranges from zero percent (interest-free access to your money) to 4.0 percent, with an average of about 1.6 percent.

If you plan to borrow extensively in the course of managing your money both within and without the variable universal life contract, you should check out both current and prospective spreads. They will affect your costs directly. And, under the new tax law, your interest on these loans will not be fully deductible.

Underwriting

In the operation of the universal variable life policy, the rate table represents the cost of insurance to be charged the buyer. Readers are familiar with the long-running public discussion of the impact of smoking on life expectancy. Regardless of the opinions of the Surgeon General or the tobacco companies, the insurers see the numbers everyday, and they do differentiate between smokers and non-smokers. A look at the rate tables will give smokers an additional incentive to chew gum or buy a yo-yo—the differences in rates between smokers and non-smokers are startling.

Rates on some policies are unisex; others are split in the traditional way between female and male insureds.

The age-range for issue is very broad, running from age 0 or 1 at the bottom, to 70, 75 and 80 at the upper end. The insurance, once purchased, covers you for the entire length of your life, of course.

The prospectus, which must be given to you in the policy presentation, contains an enormous amount of information about the contract, its operation, the various charges, and the owner's rights. It does not, however, typically provide a table of the "cost of insurance" charges that the insurer will make. The absence of hard values for this "mainspring" charge makes cost comparisons difficult to do on an item-by-item basis, as we are doing now. This difficulty is surmounted by the policy illustration, which we will come to after we have surveyed the various charges individually.

In the most popular form of the contract—the single premium—the nonmedical limits are particularly attractive. The insurers seem to have made an effort to simplify the process of applying and qualifying for single premium coverage. They are giving recognition to the real-life situation that the competitor for your premium dollar is usually a different form of pure investment, one that can be purchased simply, without passing through the underwriting process. Readers who are or were tax-shelter investors will recall that there was an analogous underwriting process, one that centered on personal finances rather than personal health.

How Charges Are Assessed

Contracts have been under design and in the field for several years now, even as the SEC regulations impacting them have been shaped and reshaped. As this is written, a revised set of such regulations is abroad and has been in existence for only a short time. The problem is one of applying existing regulatory wisdom acquired in a securities-only era, to the kind of hybrid product that constitutes variable universal life.

Many facets of existing regulations can be imported with little change; others require entirely new concepts. There has been extensive dialogue between the SEC and those who have responded to its invitation for comments. Relevant to this discussion of policy charges is the considerable flexibility that has been preserved in policy design.

Life insurers attempt in their product pricing to recapture all their expenses from all the policies they have sold and administer. In addition to this "adequacy" test, they seek to make their charges equitable—to charge each policy its fair share of the expenses of the insurer. Beyond this "equity" test, they are in competition with other carriers. Bearing in mind that you as the buyer must be given a prospectus which discloses all of the information we are talking about, and a whole lot more, the companies seek to structure their contracts so as to be appealing to the buyer and competitive with others.

It should not be surprising that great ingenuity has been displayed. Charges such as premium taxes, commission payments to salespeople, and the costs of underwriting and issuing the policy are expenses that occur at the beginning of the contract. While the language in the prospectus is difficult to follow, companies have sought to defer charging these expenses to you. Here the objective is to be able to invest all of your single premium payment initially, so it will work for you—and to be able to say so in the sales literature.

These expenses, then, are typically deferred until the second policy year and then recaptured from continuing policyholders over a period of years, say ten. The charge is made annually by the life insurer against your account value, in policy years two through eleven. It directly reduces your assets in the policy. Some people discontinue their policies, and therefore are not continuing policyholders who can be charged in future years. In this instance, the insurer simply keeps track of the amount of deferred expenses that have not been "repaid," and subtracts them from your surrender value at the time you request it.

Administrative charges are for the yearly administration of this complicated contract. They are charged against your asset value annually or monthly. There may be charges for transferring your invested funds among the several funds. Such transfers may be free for the first several transfers within a year, and charged for thereafter.

The mortality charges we discussed earlier are typically assessed monthly against the assets in your policy, the accounting being done by the insurer.

There may be charges to your account when you increase or decrease the face amount. Typically, they too are deferred and spread over a period of years after the additional face amount is issued.

The buyer pays an investment advisory fee for the management of the funds he or she has invested in the contract, and may pay for other investment expenses. These are charged to the buyer's asset account monthly. The investment advisory fee is like that which an investor in mutual funds is charged.

The variable universal life contract contains several valuable guarantees, for which the insurer makes a mortality and expense risk charge. This charge is made monthly against the assets in the buyer's account. The guarantees are that the mortality rates used to make charges to you cannot exceed the rates in a table included in the contract; and that the expense charges to you cannot be increased even if they prove to be less than the insurer's costs. The guarantee charge may include an amount designed to pay for a guarantee by the insurer that the death benefit will never be lower than a minimum guaranteed when the policy is issued.

This discussion on charges boils down to these two key points:

1. While great freedom exists in regard to charging the variable universal life buyer, most charges are made to the asset value of his investment account. If a policy terminates, charges which have been deferred are collected on the way out, from the cash surrender value.
2. It is very hard for the prospective purchaser to judge the best buy by comparing the individual expense charges. In this case, the best idea is to ask for illustrations for each policy you are interested in, and to compare the results.

Comparative Illustrations

The regulations governing variable universal life illustrations do not permit the use of any historical performance material in any way connected with funds inside the VUL. In many cases, the funds used to power the VUL are clones of free-standing mutual funds available to the public. But the companies need to provide illustrations to clarify the possible performance variations of these unusual financial instruments.

The illustration regulations now require the use of an interest rate of zero percent. Other rates are permitted; in practice, the rate most commonly illustrated is 12 percent (gross). Additionally, the material must show the gross premiums accumulated at 5 percent. This is not an illustration, but a useful measuring rod. Figure 9–2 shows a typical VUL illustration.

FIGURE 9-2
Single-Premium Variable Life Insurance Policy

Illustration of Growth Rates[1,2]

	Asset Plan		
For: John Doe Age/Sex: 40/Male Class: Nonsmoker	Guaranteed Minimum Death Benefit	Single Premium	Initial Investment Base
	149,799	50,000	50,000

Hypothetical Series Fund-Gross Yield: 12.00%

End of Policy Year	Payments[4]	Total Premiums Paid Plus Interest at 5%	Investment Base	End of Year Death Benefit[4,6]	End of Year Cash Surr Value [5,6]
1	0	52,500	54,807	162,700	51,655
5	0	63,814	79,823	222,403	76,960
10	0	81,444	128,972	320,467	128,972
15	0	103,946	212,959	458,673	212,959
20	0	132,664	349,101	658,766	349,101

Compound Annual Rates of Growth Measured from the Single Premium

End of Policy Year	Investment Base[4,6]	End of Year Death Benefit[4,6]	End of Year Cash Surr. Value[4,5,6]
5(age 45)	9.81%	32.76%	9.01%
10(age 50)	9.94%	19.56%	9.94%
15(age 55)	10.15%	15.37%	10.15%
20(age 60)	10.21%	13.35%	10.21%

FIGURE 9-2 (continued)

Illustration of Death Benefits, Cash Values and Accumulated Premiums[1,3]

For: John Doe
Age/Sex: 40/Male
Class: Nonsmoker

Asset Plan		
Guaranteed Minimum Death Benefit	Single Premium	Initial Investment Base
149,799	50,000	50,000

End of Policy Year	Payments[6]	Total Premiums Paid Plus Interest at 5%	Death Benefit[4,6] Assuming Curr. Mort. Chg. and Hypothetical Gross Annual Investment Return of:		
			0%	6.00%	12.00%
1	0	52,500	149,799	152,892	162,700
2	0	55,125	149,799	156,018	176,394
3	0	57,881	149,799	159,094	190,858
4	0	60,775	149,799	162,130	206,170
5	0	63,814	149,799	165,126	222,403
6	0	67,004	149,799	168,088	239,641
7	0	70,355	149,799	171,017	257,965
8	0	73,872	149,799	173,918	277,469
9	0	77,566	149,799	176,802	298,263
10	0	81,444	149,799	179,679	320,467
15	0	103,946	149,799	194,781	458,673
20	0	132,664	149,799	211,888	658,766
25(age 65)	0	169,317	149,799	232,294	953,521
35(age 75)	0	275,800	149,799	279,716	2,001,460

End of Policy Year	Investment Base [4,6] Assuming Curr. Mort. Chg. and Hypothetical Gross Annual Investment Return of:			Cash Surr Value [4,5,6] Assuming Curr. Mort. Chg. and Hypothetical Gross Annual Investment Return of:		
	0%	6.00%	12.00%	0%	6.00%	12.00%
1	48,820	51,814	54,807	45,668	48,661	51,655
2	47,673	53,734	60,154	43,093	49,154	55,574
3	46,532	55,737	66,065	42,525	51,730	62,057
4	45,397	57,826	72,601	41,962	54,391	69,166
5	44,267	60,003	79,823	41,405	57,140	76,960
6	43,142	62,270	87,803	40,852	59,980	85,513
7	42,022	64,630	96,616	40,305	62,913	94,899
8	40,908	67,087	106,349	39,763	65,942	105,204
9	39,799	69,646	117,098	39,227	69,073	116,526
10	38,698	72,312	128,972	38,698	72,312	128,972
15	36,062	90,436	212,959	36,062	90,436	212,959
20	33,363	112,286	349,101	33,363	112,286	349,101
25(age 65)	30,753	138,906	570,184	30,753	138,906	570,184
35(age 75)	25,089	204,108	1,460,459	25,089	204,108	1,460,459

FIGURE 9-2 (concluded)

Illustration of Death Benefits, Cash Values and Accumulated Premiums

For: John Doe
Age/Sex: 40/Male
Class: Nonsmoker

Asset Plan		
Guaranteed Minimum Death Benefit	Single Premium	Initial Investment Base
149,799	50,000	50,000

End of Policy Year	Payments[6]	Total Premiums Paid Plus Interest at 5%	Death Benefit[4,6] Assuming Guar. Mort. Chg. and Hypothetical Gross Annual Investment Return of:		
			0%	6.00%	12.00%
1	0	52,500	149,799	152,107	161,870
2	0	55,125	149,799	154,387	174,564
3	0	57,881	149,799	156,576	187,863
4	0	60,775	149,799	158,678	201,822
5	0	63,814	149,799	160,700	216,498
6	0	67,004	149,799	162,647	231,953
7	0	70,355	149,799	164,522	248,249
8	0	73,872	149,799	166,330	265,457
9	0	77,566	149,799	168,076	283,647
10	0	81,444	149,799	169,763	302,895
15	0	103,946	149,799	178,083	419,507
20	0	132,664	149,799	186,811	581,016
25(age 65)	0	169,317	149,799	195,967	804,704
35(age 75)	0	275,800	149,799	215,647	1,543,591

End of Policy Year	Investment Base[4,6] Assuming Guar. Mort. Chg. and Hypothetical Gross Annual Investment Return of:			Cash Surr Value[4,5,6] Assuming Curr. Mort. Chg. and Hypothetical Gross Annual Investment Return of:		
	0%	6.00%	12.00%	0%	6.00%	12.00%
1	48,595	51,574	54,554	45,442	48,422	51,402
2	47,218	53,220	59,577	42,638	48,640	54,997
3	45,851	54,918	65,091	41,843	50,911	61,084
4	44,492	56,668	71,142	41,057	53,233	67,707
5	43,141	58,471	77,780	40,279	55,609	74,917
6	41,800	60,328	85,059	39,510	58,038	82,769
7	40,468	62,241	93,042	38,751	60,523	91,324
8	39,147	64,210	101,795	38,002	63,065	100,650
9	37,836	66,237	111,388	37,263	65,664	110,816
10	36,534	68,321	121,900	36,534	68,321	121,900
15	32,945	82,683	194,775	32,945	82,683	194,775
20	29,392	98,997	307,899	29,392	98,997	307,899
25(age 65)	25,924	117,184	481,194	25,924	117,184	481,194
35(age 75)	19,328	157,357	1,126,354	19,328	157,357	1,126,354

[1] This is an illustration only and not a contract. Illustration for issue ages over 75 are subject to home office approval

[2] This illustration is not authorized for use unless accompanied or preceded by a prospectus and accompanied by an illustration of Death Benefits, Cash Surrender Values and Accumulated Premiums showing values for hypothetical gross rates of return of 0%, 6.00%, 12.00%. For information concerning current Net Rates of Return to Maturity which vary daily, contact the service office.

[3] Hypothetical rates of return are illustrative only and should not be deemed a representation of past or future rates of return. Actual rates of return may be more or less than those shown. The death benefit and cash surrender value for a policy would be different from those shown if actual rates of return averaged 0%, 6.00%, 12.00% over a period of years but fluctuated above or below those averages for individual policy years. No representations can be made by Crown America or the Series Fund that these hypothetical rates of return can be achieved for any one year of sustained over any period of time. This illustration must be preceded or accompanied by a current prospectus.

[4] Assumes no policy loan has been made and illustrates current cost of insurance.

[5] The cash surrender value in the first year includes a refund of 4% of the gross single premium.

[6] Includes values from additional payments, if any.

The reader can see the possibilities for dispassionate comparisons here, since each company provides software for the running of its own illustrations, and since the variable of investment performance is ruled out by the device of stipulated interest rates. Selecting common interest rates for those companies in which you are interested will permit a reasonably clean comparison of the amount and timing of the various charges to you.

Local agents and brokers can provide you with illustrations for your own situation. We recommend that you analyze these materials to get a sense of the real variations in charges that exist between companies—all in the interest of assuring yourself that you are getting a fair deal.

In summing up this chapter, it is clear that even a reasoned approach does not harness the biggest variable of all: "How will the underlying investments perform?" It is the opinion of the authors that the decision to choose a particular investment manager is the most significant one to be made by the proposed buyer, with modest differences in annual performance rates making huge differences in long-run accumulations. The concluding chapter will develop this concept.

In Summary

The reader now knows more about this new breed of insurance and mutual fund idea than the vast majority of investment and financial planning semi-professionals. A strong statement, perhaps, but true for these times.

CHAPTER 10

BUT, WHICH INVESTMENT MANAGER IS BEST FOR YOU?

"The most important thing I have ever learned about management is that the work must be done by other people."

Alfred P. Sloan, Jr., 1964

It may be hard to believe, but infinite investment returns are possible. Vincent Van Gogh might have been a mutual fund manager. However, his was a special and speculative niche in the overall investment game. Vincent painted, and less than one century ago he thought his premier canvasses might someday bring a lusty five hundred dollars or so.

"Van Gogh Brings $39.8 Million," says the Associated Press and local newspapers as we write. What once might have been pictured some decades ago as wildly overpriced at a few hundred dollars is now horrifically underpriced at forty times the sum that generally described a wealth family; a large fraction of one-hundred million dollars. Of course, Van Gogh could never have known what wonders might inure to his flashing fields. However, gold—that bright sunshine he favored so much—did indeed discover his investment stewardship. The subject of this chapter is finding that gold; the Vincent Van Gogh of mutual fund or variable life insurance that may, indeed, turn the present zircon into a diamond where your assets are at issue.

In the preceding chapters the authors have attempted to craft a series of discussions, instructions, strategies, and learned insights leading to a series of answers. That a set of answers might then lead to a solution of the overriding investment question: "How does the investor select the correct family of mutual funds, or the right variable insurance issuer?" Selection of a poor manager, we remind the reader, can be an expensive and frustrating experience.

Hopefully, many of the answers are already in hand, gleaned from the preceding chapters. Rereading the chapters on asset allocation, investment strategy, and risk and reward could be a very useful exercise.

The Van Gogh idea that began this segment is classic. For pennies you can buy the original work. For some more pennies the work trades (sells to someone else) in the art network. An art lover comes along and discovers the merit of that great person's work. The price soars for all of Vincent's work, and all art related to his time and afterward also appreciates in value.

Can you, the modern mutual fund investor, find the Vincent Van Gogh of stock and bond management in the overwhelming expansion occurring in mutual funds today, and the profusion of life insurance products meant to mimic these?

Can you, the reader, comfortably deal with the stock broker or financial planner—the folks who rightly charge for their time? Is it possible to merely plunk down a few dollars and study the recommendations contained in the proliferating mutual fund advisories? Can you glean significant stuff from the less expensive tabloids and slick investment monthlies? Can you, the investor, go it alone? After all, a latter-day U.S. Senator from the great state of New Hampshire announced, in his time, that that approach—throwing darts at the list of choices—was correct and effective!

THE WINNING HAND

Our friend Bob Dik announced in an earlier chapter, "Find the face cards of investment and you will win the hand." Weeks, our man of rivers, salmon, and authors would agree. However, finding the correct fly, the ideal water to fish, and ideal overall conditions in Mother Nature's world are difficult at best. Remember: it is always your money! Brokers, financial planners, other varieties of advisors, newsletter gurus, and bankers often forget that very simple economic fact—the money belongs to somebody else, and we earn our pay dealing with that money!

Selection of the appropriate mutual fund or insurance company manager is not the only thing, it is everything. In earlier chapters, we have attempted to skillfully make the case for manager selection and strategy choice. Considering the heady nature of the subject—"How does the reader select the family of funds?"—we propose the following: rereading of prior text.

No answers are ever obvious. The only elements in the process that equate with the word obvious are those that are clearly understood. "Is that point, tool, strategy, concept, or idea now obvious?" When the reader can say yes instead of no, progress in the battle for investment-and-savings survival has indeed been made.

NOT SO OBVIOUS ANSWERS ... PLUS OBVIOUS QUESTIONS

1. First, you are interested in and convinced about the modern mutual fund family. This set of investment mechanics is either the way to go, or the thing to avoid.

The writers firmly believe that the modern mutual fund family is a winning approach. Of course there are the variable insurance products, and the highly leveraged wonders of Wall Street that you might speculate with. When the chips are being tallied, we believe that more winners will be found in mutual funds than elsewhere in the financial services and Wall Street complex.

Said another way, the percentage of winners as opposed to the other nasty experience will be higher for mutual fund shareowners than for investors in unmanaged portfolios of common stocks. If the winning ratio is higher for fund holders versus direct stockholders by a huge margin, then the ratio for fund holders versus players in the options, commodity futures, and penny stock arenas will be immense.

2. When tax considerations are weighed the choices become the stand-alone and taxable mutual fund, the tax free bond departments of mutual funds, or such tax shading alternatives as are found in the life insurance sector— VL/VUL.

Heady and often boggling stuff: mutual fund and asset manager selection is all of that. When tax considerations play a part as well, the symphony involves fewer keys on the piano and shorter strings on the violin.

3. Strategies have been discussed herein. Some of these are new, such as those in the "D" series, while others are well tried and tested.

Winners and losers can be discovered when any strategy is employed, or when any statistical summary is displayed. Investment results must always be viewed in terms of "what if?" There are no magic tricks in the previous pages. This is true for mutual fund family managers as well as the new variable insurance clones for these funds. "Buy-and-hold" will always work for those who purchase at the correct time. The "dollar-cost-averaging" game will work whenever the disciplined program is begun, at least in the eyes of these observers. Dollar-cost-averaging just requires time and, of course, a steely discipline.

We firmly believe the "D" series of packaged approaches is sheer poetry, profit dynamite. But hard questions remain. Which is the correct investment strategy, and where is the best management to shepherd your money? The question is much more difficult to deal with now than just a few years back. The consulting firm, Arthur D. Little, when doing some planning work for a Boston-based mutual fund sponsor in the late 1970s, surfaced only 18 families of funds in the load area. Today there are ten times as many, and the number continues to grow by leaps and bounds.

4. Sector and niche funds are hot topics. Either they will play a key role in your thinking or the more traditional broadly diversified funds will be the right answer.

Sector fund selection further complicates the management selection question. The majority of sector funds are found with one manager, Fidelity. Possibly—since sector funds for most investors will likely be a minor part of their overall strategy— the conventional broadly based funds also managed by that sponsor will not be those that you find comfort with.

We believe these specialty products are a phenomenon related to the confusion caused by the tireless bull market in stocks. Everybody seems bent on the difficult and profitless effort of gaining ground on those few stock market and mutual fund players who "toughed it out" when the stock market was not rising.

The world of savers and investors is not without its clear winners. The winners were patient and tough, and they believed in America, and in growth and professional investment management through mutual fund ownership. The "niche fund players" may experience a special discovery usually assigned to the losers: unanticipated tax losses.

5. And, most important, a basic judgement has been made by now about risk tolerance. Each reader is mentally positioned at some confortable or reasonable point on the capital-market line in risk and reward terms. Expected or anticipated investment rewards are neither too high or too low.

When taking risk of any type, being safe is always better than being sorry. In Figure 10–1, the reader will see where 101 percent of the saving and investing public is placed along the capital-market line. The vast majority of this public is placed at or near zero risk, in such instruments as savings accounts, bank certificates of deposit, money market, and government or quality corporate and tax-exempt bond mutuals.

Fewer than 20 percent seem willing to accept normal market risk as found in blue chip and quality growth common stocks, or the mutual funds managed in that risk zone. And an even smaller percentage—14 percent—displays a willingness to shoot for half of the norm: beta .50–.70.

The shock in Figure 10–1 is that there seem to be no speculators. We wonder how the hotels in Atlantic City or Las Vegas

FIGURE 10–1
Distribution of Investors Along the Market Line

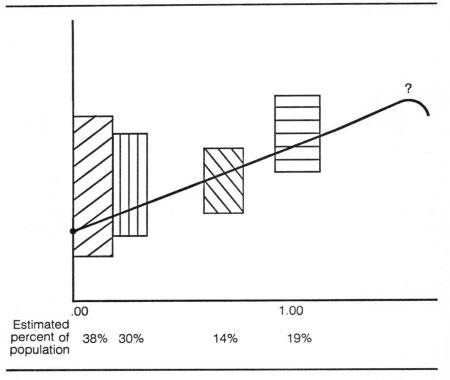

Estimated
percent of   38%   30%   14%   19%
population

Source: Northmark Financial Services©

get filled, and who buys all of those lottery tickets that the states print with abandon. Where does the heavy volume of trading in over-the-counter markets come from? Or how can really speculative markets—Salt Lake City, Vancouver, Toronto, for example—survive without speculators!

    6. Finally, the reader believes in America and the free-enterprise economic system in the free world.

Without a yes answer, mutual funds that buy and hold common stocks are probably not a correct answer for savings and investment. Neither are bank accounts or life insurance values.

The banking system and the insurance industry are indeed built on the foundation of investments that mirror free enterprise.

Possibly the only correct mutual fund answers for those readers who do not believe in the system as presently constituted lie in funds that own gold-mining companies (the end is near) or invest only in bonds issued and guaranteed by Uncle Sam.

THERE IS NO REASONABLE DOUBT

The families, worldwide, that have built and sustained great fortunes know the answers to the management question posed earlier. The modern Boeskys make it and give it back. The venturer to Las Vegas and the lottery ticket line do much the same. There is little substance in the make-it-today stance. Real money is usually made by those investors with great discipline and greater patience. Once the money is made by being smart, continuing to operate as a smart investor becomes easier or less troublesome.

Let us continue with our series of major points. These are not "Ten Commandments," but humble stuff that derives from a combined 60 years of success and failure. Sixty years is roughly the past life for mutual funds in America, and ten times the effective life for the modern mutual fund family and variable insurance clones.

7. A decision has been made to "do it yourself." This implies use of no-load mutual funds. After all, why would you use a load fund if the decisions for success or failure rest exclusively with you rather than the stock broker or financial planner charging you a commission, or a financial counseling firm to which you are paying a fee?

In the guise of management or fund family selection the question is moot and the answer a ho-hum. We are hardly certain that the time-tested argument for load versus no-load mutual funds even exists. As noted in Chapters 1 and 2, the game is changing as fast as the salmon's strike at the fly.

- No-load was once surely that: no charge. The investor paid zero in sales levies to come aboard. A typical management fee was exacted each year the fund or funds were held; and, under the then prevailing structures, another zero charge was assessed when the fund shares were sold or exchanged.
- A load fund, with that storied 8 percent charge, related to a far different set of circumstances, at least according to the media and public mindset: "Those poor buggers sure paid up for that!"

Not true at all, at least in an active sense. First, the dreaded 8 percent load was charged on smaller sales only—typically $25,000 or less, and in some cases $10,000 or less. A huge and growing number of purchases these days are $100,000 or larger. These typically carry a sales charge of 3 percent or less. In most instances the charge is "round-trip" in design, which means it covers both the buy and sell sides of the transaction. And, presumably, the charge was generated when the fund purchaser accepted selection or timing advice from a qualified sales representative.

That latter point should not be swept under the rug. As we saw in Chapter 9, there are some very persuasive ideas that affect millions of families. The financial aid applications that may possibly reduce college tuition expenses is one that applies to almost 50 million teen and pre-teen children. RICO and the malpractice applications for protecting assets from the courts apply to a smaller audience. However, these three ideas were generated through the broker and financial-planning communities, not the no-load mutual fund sponsors.

Thus the question really is not load versus no-load. It becomes a logical issue only in terms of the value of services rendered. Is a 5 percent sales charge (call that $1,500 on a $30,000 variable life purchase) expensive or cheap if the tuition savings add up to $15,000 over the four-year college cycle? It seems to the authors that it equates to a return of 1,000 percent!

It would be more than a little difficult for any comparison of actual investment results to be tallied for the long term—say, two decades or longer—where the "do-it-yourself" investor would not find actual investment results close for the good no-load fund and the bad load fund. As we noted in earlier chapters, the annual fees charged by no-load funds tend to be a bit higher than for load funds. Over long periods this higher continuing fee can sometimes offset the drag of the load or sales charge.

Load fund groups such as American Funds, Pioneer, Massachusetts Investors Trust, Keystone, Putnam, and others have long-term track records that sparkle. Similarly, Scudder Stevens & Clark (Weeks' favorite during the years of the Great Crash), Loomis Sayles, Northeast Investors Trust, T. Rowe Price, and other notable no-load fund groups have similarly spectacular investment records.

The argument—load versus no-load in manager or fund family selection—comes down to a series of key points. For our purposes, use the term "timing." To expand on that term, also use the idea that strong and timely communication between the mutual fund sponsor and the shareholder is essential to a successful investment and savings program.

- Did the world of mutual funds exist prior to the advent of full-page mutual fund advertising in the slick media?
- Were mutual funds widely known (rather than being widely understood) prior to the beginnings of the great bull market in stocks that began in the 1980s?

If mutual funds in both categories were known and understood, why didn't more families, retirement plans, and other conscious investors find them? Since both classes of fund (load and no-load) existed, why do the total returns earned look so much alike when multi-decade periods are measured? The authors have never met one unhappy mutual fund shareholder where ownership has gone beyond twenty years, be the fund load or no-load!

To take the management selection process further in this river of opportunity, we bring up the people question. People generally underperform in terms of total return because they leave assets in bank savings accounts and penuriously compensated accounts with life insurers. Why? Nobody told them to do anything different! The mutual funds—good, bad and best—were not highly visible at market bottoms in the mid-1970s, because media costs were simply too high.

A favorite line of the folks who use the capital-market line—as discussed in-depth in the chapter on risk and reward—goes, "The market is efficient—that is, always priced correctly on the basis of all known information. It is the people, the investing public, that are inefficient." We clearly see that in action today. As an example, the purchases of bond and other safe mutual funds outdistance purchases of stock and growth funds by a margin of nearly three to one, even after a huge and sustained bull market in common stocks.

However, banks were talking about risk avoidance with their full-page advertisements. Life insurers were barking about premium returns. Coin and stamp dealers—examples of a general class of purveyors of collectables—were stalking the marketplace with gloom and doom as their story. Purveyors of tax shelters of all varieties were buying space in all variety of media to tell their tax-avoidance-shelter story: "Send us your money and we will have Uncle Sam pay all the bills!" All the while, mutual fund families said very little.

Since the chips fall wherever they will, and fall regularly, it seems, on those steeped in inaction and confusion, having sage counsel on questions such as "when?" or "why?" gains more than just a bit of importance. We have no particular brief for either the load or no-load fund as a best answer. The points being made vis-à-vis management selection relate only to people, timing, and ideas!

- You, the present or potential mutual fund investor, need to know the answer to "when."
- Knowing the "when" answer leads inevitably to the equally important "why."
- Timing for these crucial answers is equal to "Z"—the results you might earn over time from the mutual fund family chosen.

Now that we have these issues behind us, we can move forward to the selection issue. In Chapters 1 and 2, we covered many of the angles that could lead you to the correct selection answer. In the chapter on risk and reward, we delivered important tools that should be useful in augmenting and strengthening the selection procedure for the fund family or variable insurance product.

There is little doubt, in our minds at least, that the huge growth in sheer numbers of fund families will lead to a shakeout of the lessor lights as this bull market peaks, as all have in the past, and turns into a roaring bear market. There simply are not enough top-quality asset managers, and stock and bond analysts to staff these thousands of new funds and hundreds of new sponsor organizations.

With your money on the line, being second best is the same thing as losing the race. While no mutual funds have gone broke, as far as these authors know, many once-popular mutual fund names—particularly ones from the "Go-Go" growth years of the 1960s—were tarnished badly by the subsequent bear markets in the 1970s. Some of these are mere shadows of past glories. Some never fully recovered, and investment results (and shareholders) suffered. We expect a repeat performance—a shakeout coupled with some really dismal investment results—when the bull ceases to snort on Wall Street.

BIG IS GOOD

The authors made the point in previous chapters that "big" can be very important where mutual funds and variable life insurance products are concerned. Big, in this context, relates to the aggregate sum under management or control. A multi-billion-dollar, high-beta growth fund may be bad, as we noted earlier, since with each additional dollar to manage, it becomes more difficult to manage.

However, in terms of the full complement of funds—the total of all moneys managed in all funds or insurance separate accounts—big is akin to wonderful. After all, the fund management lives largely on the management fees earned from the funds themselves. Two critical points:

1. The people who actually manage the fund portfolios are expensive if they are good—if they have glowing track

records. The young securities analysts being trained to be tomorrow's portfolio managers are likely to come from the most important and prestigious graduate schools. Generally at the top of their class, these professionals are expensive to buy and maintain.

The large fund and insurance organizations—those with large fund families and huge management-fee income—have a far better chance of both attracting and keeping the proven managers and analysts. These groups also act as a magnet at the top graduate schools, attracting the cream of the crop because of reputation and financial muscle.

We are not suggesting that smallish or new mutual funds are imperfect or tainted in any way. There are entrepreneurs on Wall Street as well as in high-technology. Great fund managers from time to time will slip away from the clutches of bigness, opting for a company of their own. Gerry Tsai, Fidelity Funds' wizard in the early 1960s, is a case in point. He left to form the Manhattan Fund, which was successfully underwritten by Wall Street brokerages and subsequently sold to Chicago's CNA Financial.

The key point in management selection is that where a small or new fund is being reviewed, a very important step is to determine the track record of the actual fund manager prior to joining that small or new fund. If that record is moribund or spotty, you have the answer—move on with your investigations.

2. Mutual fund and variable account management is information-intensive. The managers live on the flow of stock, interest rate, market, and economic research.

The timeliness and quality of the research delivered to the fund family is critical to tomorrow's investment results—the total returns that may be earned by the investor. The fund managers and analysts simply cannot follow every stock and bond on an intimate, hands-on, daily basis.

Thus the analysts and portfolio managers rely heavily on third-party information sources. Weighing heavily in importance as quality sources are the research departments of larger Wall

Street investment banks, and regional brokerages. If the fund manager needs to know something about the economy and opportunities in Atlanta, a call to Robinson-Humphrey is in order. If the fund is interested in Europe, investment banks such as Morgan Stanley and Goldman Sachs might be brought in for discussions.

The big mutual funds and life insurers have millions in commission dollars that can be used to pay for these favors. These goliaths also have the considerable management fees that might be used in part to pay for the attention they need from consulting firms, independent economists, and other third-party information sources.

It would be patently unfair to both Wall Street and these huge fund families to suggest that the big groups get all of the best information, or get important data before any of the smaller groups hear the story. However, there is little question in your authors' minds that a certain favoritism is in play in this regard.

After all, the largest sources of data are the Wall Street giants. These firms work for commissions. Thus they are prone to look at the larger mutual fund sponsors and life insurance companies as being productive of more and larger commissions than the smaller firms.

The larger sponsors, with few exceptions, also have a broader variety of offerings for their investors. The cost of starting new mutual funds is not cheap. For the life insurance companies starting variable life and universal variable life product lines, the costs are simply stupendous.

The break-even point for a new fund started today is a larger number than was paid for the Van Gogh painting cited at the beginning of the chapter. Therefore, in addition to the sizeable start-up costs, the sponsor is faced with potentially heavy marketing expenses to achieve break-even.

For large mutual fund families and huge insurance organizations, the break-even problem is a small one. These giants are supported by huge management fees and have considerable financial muscle. If the new fund doesn't reach break-even, they can merge the fund with another in their stable at fairly small cost.

Thus, big is good in a broad sense, for those readers making first-time selection decisions. The great management names, which include both load and no-load fund sponsors, have people power, research and information clout, and financial guns that can work in your favor.

RESULTS, RESULTS, RESULTS

In the end, however, the most important determining factor is found in the results earned in the past, and hoped for in the future. Many new funds and new fund families—and in all cases, variable separate investment accounts—lack a prior management record.

In some cases, as noted elsewhere, the new fund or variable product groups have made arrangements with established and skillful managers. We noted that earlier when making reference to the IDEX series (Janus Capital), the new Sass*Southmark funds (M.D. Sass), and International Heritage (Vanguard, Endowment, Lombard-Odier).

Under existing federal regulations, these new mutual fund families are now allowed to publish the past results for these managers as being their own. But the records are there for all to see. Publications at the public library—*Pension World* and *Pension Investment Age,* for example—carry regular comparisons for those as well as other firms that manage the huge retirement plans and endowment funds.

We also made a case for the Rightime Fund. Here, although the fund is just two years of age as we write, the manager does not buy stocks and bonds, but instead uses shares of other proven mutual funds as the investment approach. Thus, Rightime—a fund of funds—uses the services of those same huge mutual fund managers that we dealt with earlier.

THE GAME: INVESTMENT CONSISTENCY

Since nobody can predict the future with any reliability, the first inning in the management selection ballgame is devoted to the study of previous results. As noted earlier, reliance on immediate past performance is a dangerous affair where mutual fund selection is the game. The year or quarter just concluded can be very misleading. Like all humans, fund portfolio managers can experience the joys of luck, at least on a short-range basis where stock selection and investment strategy games are being played.

Conversely, if the mutual fund being studied has been around for more than ten years—and, hopefully, alive during the great bear market of the early and mid-1970s—a string of five- and ten-year comparisons can be developed. These, if the fund is fifteen years of age or more, will include both good markets and terrible ones.

1. How did the fund perform relative to its peers in the chain of good markets, and bull or rising markets?
2. How did the fund perform relative to its peers in the markets that either began or concluded on a sour note; a bear or declining market?
3. Overall, when measured against a grouping of funds with similar investment objectives, was the fund in the top quartile (the top 25 percent) in terms of total returns delivered? If a stock or growth fund is generally in the top quartile against the competition for five five-year periods, it will almost always be found in the top 10 percent for the entire period.

Those are the "ABCs" for performance evaluation on a general basis. Consistency is everything. Consistent performers attract the finest and most qualified analysts and managers. They also retain the moneys under management for longer periods, which adds incrementally to their profits. The reader, we believe, knows now that the profits for the manager of the mutual fund or life insurer work powerfully to motivate good future investment results.

Figure 10–2 demonstrates that variable products, despite higher carrying costs, produce slightly better long-term results. The absence of taxes is the reason. The conclusion of this line of reasoning is clear, or should be. First, recent investment results should be counted as misleading and possibly flawed. Longer-term results should be broken down into market time segments—five, ten, or even fifteen years—and the results compared with similar types of mutual funds with similar invest-

FIGURE 10–2
Comparison of Investment Total Returns:
Variable Annuities versus Taxable Mutual Funds

Variable Annuities Edge Out Funds

The equivalent after-tax annual rate of return for tax-deferred annuities slightly exceeds that of mutual funds, assuming a 12 percent total return before expenses and taxes. But, Glenn S. Daily of Seidman Financial Services cautions, one's wealth at retirement will be determined far more by the investment performance of the funds within the variable annuity than by tax deferment.

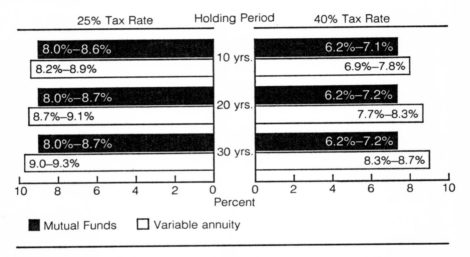

Source: *New York Times* Financial Planning Guide, Sunday, November 16, 1986. Copyright 1986 by The New York Times Company. Reprinted by permission.

ment goals. After all, the modern mutual fund family can be a cradle-to-grave experience . . . and a very productive one if the correct family or variable fund manager is discovered.

THE SECRET WEAPON

In Chapter 4, as well as elsewhere in the book, the authors developed measurement tools for readers that might be called "the secret weapon in management selection." The key word is *alpha*. The measurement tool is found in the capital market line, or *beta*.

All mutual funds and variable separate accounts can be measured as to previous total returns. These results, coupled with the beta or risk to which the fund was exposing the shareholders' assets, deliver a cryptic and starkly simple picture of past and present management skill. The key question is: Is the manager delivering the beta promise, or less than that? If less, fire the manager and hire a better one!

If the portfolio manager is producing plus alpha—more return than indicated by the risk exposure in the portfolio—send that manager more money to manage. It is quite that simple. You are buying results with your money. You have determined your personal risk tolerance. You have developed a risk target that suits you. Mutual funds tracking at or above the beta number represent good news. Those struggling to stay on the beta line, or those slipping below that line, are bad news. Avoid these and you will be a happier shareholder, making money.

THOSE STRANGE VARIABLE LIFE OPTIONS

As noted in Chapters 8 and 9, the variable life insurance policies are mutual funds in disguise, and can be measured tomorrow in the same fashion used for conventional taxable mutual funds. However, there are some fairly important differences, and as we moved through the chapters on variables we attempted to make note of some of those differences.

The major ones relate to the fact that life insurance is, by law and regulation, part of each of these policies, except for the variable annuity. The life insurance element is not provided free! Thus the alpha-beta capital-market-line method of selection is fuzzed by this built-in set of mortality expenses—the life insurance premium.

Next, unlike conventional mutuals which provide the bookkeeping as a part of the expense ratio or management fee, the life insurance industry has opted for separate charges that are levied against the policy asset—the disguised, nontaxable mutual fund.

Thus this combination of direct expenses must be adjusted into the calculation of beta, and then adjusted again for the tax savings. The authors referred to this in previous chapters as "drag." Said another way, the net effect is that these expenses absolutely reduce total investment return. For most purchasers, however, the tax savings on various income streams, now sheltered from taxation, should, over time, easily compensate for the reduced return.

THE PRINT ADVISORY SERVICES

Of course, readers can skip over all of our suggestions and subscribe to one of the plethora of fee advisories which are more than willing to add your name to their subscription list. If that suits you, go to it.

You may try subscribing to one or more of these, and then checking the advisories-selection record using the alpha-beta techniques. Remember, these good folks are in business to sell hard copy and advice for a fee. Has that advice, in picking a good mutual fund or fund family, been superb, good, mediocre, or flawed? Indeed, does a back record of recommendations even exist?

Van Gogh and the sale of his painting for many pennies less than $40 million began this chapter. It is of note that that great painter sold exactly one painting during his lifetime. Of this recent sale for mega-millions, one observer in the press noted that if the sale were in "real money, the price would have been 5.8 billion yen!"

With that thought in mind, we move on to the issue of tomorrow. Change is in the wind, and the gusts of change would boggle the ability of a modern wind machine to harness the energy.

PART 3

CONCLUSIONS

CHAPTER 11

MUTUAL FUNDS & VARIABLE LIFE PROXIES: THE FUTURE

"I never invest in anything that eats or requires repairing."

Billy Rose

A very tall order indeed. Where is the mutual fund industry headed? Where are the securities markets going? What additional product and pricing evolution will occur? How will the tax-code authors in Washington react to that evolution? When the tax magic of the new variable insurance products is considered from the perspective of the federal deficits, their future be the largest and most difficult question of all.

However, the first order of business is to deal with the stock and bond market. Quite a lot has happened since one of the authors concluded his book, *Andersen on Mutual Funds* (Scott, Foresman, 1984), with a prediction: "In fact, this decade will see a dramatic revival of interest in financial instruments of all kinds (stocks, bonds and therefore mutual funds among them) as the transition to a new generation of technology occurs successfully."

Following that, in *Andersen on Financial Planning* (Dow Jones-Irwin, 1986), this was the forecast: "And the new tax law is clearly playing into the hands of (my) bullish scenario . . . the coming boom in stock prices will be good news for properly positioned families." In other words, in both instances, owners of common stocks, long maturity bonds, and the mutual funds that invest in these will prosper.

We continue to be quite bullish on the market despite the tremendous rise in stock prices. Therefore, we are bullish also on well-managed mutual fund and variable life investments, as these will mirror or exceed results achieved by the popular market indices. We readily subscribe to the Wall Street adage that "no tree grows to the sky." Bull markets, as we have noted throughout this book, are indeed always followed by bear markets! However, the present raging bull—approaching 2400 on the Dow as we write—will be no exception to that rule. History and market realities also appear to support the idea that prices for stocks have a lot more room on the upside, and that interest rates should be even lower before this period of disinflation ends.

Since we feel that interest rates will continue lower—good news for owners of quality bond mutual funds—Figure 11–1 is appealing. Published by Harold Gourgues, author of "The Gourgues Report" and financial-planning expert, Figure 11–1 addresses to what happens to the stock market when interest rates bottom. His work indicates that when the bottom in interest rates is reached, using 20-year government bonds as the measuring stick, stocks will continue to rise, on average, for another 30 percent or so.

Thus, putting the calculator to the present market and the Gourgues study, and assuming that interest rates will bottom

FIGURE 11–1

When Interest Rates Bottom in Bull Markets, Stocks Continue to Gain an Average 30.2%

		S&P 500			Rates Bottomed in Week Ending:	Next Market High:	Number of Elapsed Months:
	20-Year Govt Low	Week's Close	Next High	% Gain			
	2.58	29.83	49.74		Aug '54	Aug 2 '56	24
	3.17	43.44	60.71	39.8%	Apr '58	Aug 3 '59	16
	3.84	56.96	72.64	27.5%	Aug '60	Dec 12 '61	16
	4.48	86.07	108.37	25.9%	Jan 21 '67	Nov 29 '68	23
	5.79	94.46	120.24	27.3%	Nov 6 '71	Jan 11 '73	14
	7.23	107.46	111.27	3.5%	Jan 1 '77	Oct 5 '79	34
	9.59	114.06	140.52	23.2%	June 21 '80	Nov 28 '80	5
	10.52	134.90	172.65	28.0%	Nov 27 '82	Oct 10 '83	11
Thus far:	7.33	242.38	245.67		Apr 19 '86	June 6 '86	2
If average gain were applied now:		315.00	30.2%			Oct '87	18

Source: The Gourgues Report.

in 1987, a Dow Jones Industrial average north of 3100 would be a logical target. Some points to consider:

1. The present bull market has been virtually impervious to political or economic events, as documented by the Iranian arms scuffle, spying by Israel, and the Contra aid snafus.
2. Price inflation, despite all of the worrying, seems well under control at "manageable" levels as the economy remains weak to limp, and industrial commodities and farm prices drift lower. Only in health care, tuition costs, and related service areas do we find persistent price increases.
3. Absence of large doses of price inflation forces interest rates, over time, to ever-lower levels. This, in turn, makes common stock and blue chip and growth mutual fund "total returns"—dividends plus capital gains—more attractive to a growing audience of risk takers.
4. The sheer volume of assets allocated both here and abroad to cash-like investments, earning ever lower returns from money market and short-term debt instruments, bodes well for stock prices and mutual fund values.
5. The supply of stocks available for investor purchase has actually been shrinking since the late 1970s because of buy-backs and leveraged buy-out operations. There are more dollars available to purchase stocks, but there are fewer shares to buy!

The combination of macro factors above is incredibly bullish for the financial markets. Also, a look at market history seems to make a powerful analogy between present stock market price action and the huge bull market that occurred in the 1912–29 period.

That great bull market began in 1912 with the Dow Jones Industrials trading in a range of 80 to 94. The comparable year for the present bull market was 1971: the Dow average at that time was 798 to 951. From that beginning forward there has been a clear "ten-times" relationship year-to-year with the earlier period (see Figure 11–2).

In 1928 the Dow rose to 300. In 1929 the average hit a top of 381. If researchers were to explore the front pages of the *Wall*

FIGURE 11–2
**Dow Jones Industrial Average: Price Ranges for the Present and
Previous Bull Market**

Year	Range	Year	Range
1915	57-99	1974	578-892
1924	88-121	1983	1027-1287
1926	135-167	1985	1185-1553
1927	153-202	1986	1530-2020!

Street Journal and *New York Times* for that period, they would find the same headlines as today: problems with Russia, a weak industrial economy, a terrible farm situation, etc. Should the "ten-times" ratios continue, the Dow Jones Industrials will reach 3800+ before some unknown series of forces chops the top off the market tree!

Fortunes can and likely will be made before that obvious and predictable downturn occurs. Those readers who employ the lessons in this book—remembering that a bull market climbs a wall of worry—will prosper using the alpha-beta techniques to monitor investment performance. The simple device of beta and the capital-market line will allow the reader to discover the best mutual fund family and variable life asset managers, and employ the "D" series of investment strategies and market timing to control risk and undue market exposure.

PRODUCTS AND SERVICES: WHAT'S GOING TO BE NEW?

As we noted in earlier chapters, the new product-innovation factory on Wall Street, asset management, banking, and life insurance have been working double overtime in this decade. Possibly more products and services for savers and investors have been invented, reinvented, or redesigned in any recent year than in any previous decade. Readers will recall that the shape of mutual funds from 1924 and 1964 remained much the same: blue chip, balanced, and income funds.

As the present markets continue in their super-bull trend, millions of new investors will be attracted to mutual funds and the recently added variable life insurance proxies. This massive injection of new money will stimulate equally massive amounts of creativity and repackaging from a variety of product sources.

As repressive federal and state laws and regulations weaken, commercial banks and thrift depositories will become major, if not *the* major participants in this evolutionary product boom. These institutions, we recall, were the king-makers of the market boom in the 1920s. In this evolutionary product boom, they will relearn the games forgotten since the Bank Holiday in 1933, and subsequent passage of the Glass-Steagal Act and the various securities laws that swept them into the corners of Wall Street. But this will take time, as banks tend to move with more than modest caution.

Product innovation to date, as we saw in Chapter 2 and the chapters covering variable life insurance, has been a combination of reinvention (sector funds, for example) and true invention related to changing tax law. Many of the tools created by Wall Street and mutual fund sponsors—option income funds and hedged bond funds using financial futures and puts and calls, for example—are indeed new. However, new is not always necessarily good.

Thus we would expect that the mutual fund industry, the variable life insurance sector of that industry, other asset managers attempting to enter the arena, and stock brokerage firms will continue to evolve new or reworked products for all classes and types of investors. A tongue-in-cheek comment from a recent issue of *Barron's* tells it all: "Is there, as of 1987, one mutual fund, investing in some specific (market) sector, for every man, woman and child in the United States?" Consider reinvention or repackaging of mutual funds with reference to the era of the 1920s described in Figure 11–2.

- Closed-end funds have blossomed again of late. Recent and present activity has focused primarily in the country fund and utility area. Because of early success with billion-dollar offerings that often traded at premium prices, this activity will spread to other industries (think sector funds) and appear in new shapes and structures using hedging tools, financial leverage, and other esoterica. Shades of the Roaring Twenties!

- The "duo-fund"—a mutual fund with two classes of investor, one owning all income, and the other all of the price or capital-gain potential—is coming back after two decades of painful investor forgetfulness. Shades of the "Go-Go" years!

- The "competitive asset manager" idea—another repeat performance of what did not work well in the 1960s—is also emerging again. In this unique type of mutual fund, the fund employs multiple investment managers. The manager who manages best for the recent periods—good alpha-beta results—gets new money to manage, while the manager who performs poorly gets none. Shades of investing logic turned upside down!

Is there true innovation in the wings? Of course! Wall Street never sleeps when there are as many chips on the table for investment as there are now. After all, mutual fund sponsors, life insurers, banks, and other institutions that package things for investors are in business to make money by gaining a measure of control over the reader's money!

While there are a few "funds-of-funds" in the marketplace today such as Rightime Fund, before this bull market runs out of gas readers will see dozens more. Some will be focused on a specific industry, others will offer to manage the growing list of sector funds, and still others will likely add an element of borrowing by the mutual fund to spice the total returns possible with leverage. Thinking back to the 1929–33 period, excessive use of leverage was both cause and effect.

Mutual funds that specialize in purchasing and owning "initial public offerings" (IPOs)—typically untried and untested companies—will appear. A bull market of this magnitude for stocks will likely not conclude without an explosion in public interest in the new-stock-issue-underwriting game; the IPO scenario.

After all, only a small percentage of potential investors has prospered from the stock market liftoff in 1983 at the Dow Industrials 1000 level. Thus, multitudes will attempt to play "catch-up" with new stock issues and other speculative approaches. And, of course, most of these folks will lose rather than win because of the incredible beta exposures that walk arm-in-arm with speculation. Readers will recall from the alpha-beta discussion and the capital-market line that there is a point beyond which taking risk simply is not logical or productive.

Thus as far as the modern mutual family goes—both the open-end garden variety and closed-end format—the innovative forces in financial services will be thrusting against ever more speculative and narrow-purpose funds. Who needs a new pure-vanilla growth fund?

With thousands of mutual funds in place today—many of the old, tested, and proven variety such as bond, growth, blue chip, balanced, income, and total return—the innovators will roll the dice in a progressively casino-style atmosphere. The fund and insurance sponsors, looking for money to manage, want to cater to the army of well-heeled but not well-trained new players. The results, when the market tree is trimmed from the top down, will be much the same as the phenomenon witnessed in hotel lobbies and airport lounges in Las Vegas (a city we refer to as "Lost Wages") and Atlantic City: dour and dismal!

All too many asset managers and brokerage firms are greedy for the investor dollar, at whatever cost. Life insurers see a flood of fee and premium income coming from variable life. Brokerage firms see a bottom-line profit source coming from house-sponsored mutual fund families that did not exist in prior bear markets. "When the mail man has a hump on his back from carrying in the checks," as one senior officer of a mutual fund sponsor opined, "business is good."

Good business is often at the expense of the saver and investor when disaster strikes down the road. A good example of this negative effect comes from the life insurance and annuity industry. There was a time when buyers flocked to purchase single premium annuities. Stock brokers raced to the marketplace to sell these annuities. Baldwin United gleefully responded, and in due course was found to have offered interest-rate guarantees that were unrealistically high. These rates were bankrupting the life insurance company!

When something looks too good to be true, count on it, it is! But with the explosion of Madison Avenue marketing approaches on Wall Street, and the heady bull market for stocks that finds most of the money still in cash and still on the sidelines, the trend in pure product innovation will lean heavily toward speculative answers.

No doubt experienced mutual fund families—those with huge assets under management and decades of experience that were suggested to readers in Chapter 10—will become involved in the speculative new product binge. But they will remain as the proven mutual fund suppliers that will, as a brokerage friend commented, "Live to fight another day!" Two conclusions:

1. The market of stocks is poised to go quite a lot higher. In that process, huge sums both here and abroad will shift from low-yielding bonds and money market instruments to the allure of higher total returns available from common stocks. The way to play the stock market is spelled "mutual fund family" and "variable universal life insurance."
2. Product innovation will turn progressively more speculative as both the fund and insurance sponsor attempt to capture assets from the hordes of new investors rushing to cash in on the bull market.

Clear symptoms of worrisome conclusion two are seen in recent moves by the Fidelity Group to offer "short sale" facilities for speculators through its discount brokerage operation. A short sale involves selling a security that the investor expects to decline in price. Such a sale—in this case, shares of a mutual fund— is a leveraged transaction since the potential for loss is infinite. Short sales also cause interest payments to be made; or, if dividends are declared and paid by the fund, the liability rests with the short seller.

Equally risky is the quiet approval by the Federal Reserve Board of the offering of mutual funds on margin. In this case, the investor might use existing shares held as collateral for a loan from a broker to buy more shares. The logic is that if the price is going to double, why not own twice as many shares. That is clearly leveraging the play. However, markets also go down, and that means losing money twice as fast!

To render the short sale and margin purchase of mutual funds even more risky, the interest charges are no longer a deductible business expense. Thus the mutual fund shares that are sold short can go up in price, and the shares leveraged on margin can go down. In both events a loss is recorded. That loss is expanded by the amount of interest paid to carry the account.

A major discount broker, Charles Schwab & Company, reported that of the $4 billion worth of fund transactions processed in 1986, one-third were in margin accounts. Other discount brokers have reported higher percentages of fund sales on margin. In one case, the ratio was two-thirds of all sales.

VARIABLE LIFE INSURANCE OFFERINGS

While many of the life insurers now offering variable contracts began these with very basic investment weapons—cash fund, bond fund, balance, and blue chip or growth fund—positioned along the capital market line, innovation will strike these more conservative folks as well. After all, these variable policies will be much easier to sell because of the tax angle. Since these insurers are learning about higher-risk equity investment, but are not directly on the hook for lost value as they would be in conventional policies, readers are going to see a much higher level of speculative product introduced by this class of sponsor. How quickly these folks forget the problems caused, as noted earlier in this chapter, by offering something unrealistic: Whether it be profit-stunting commissions to salespeople, or returns on investment that logically cannot be earned.

Investment options configured in these new variable policies will be expanded to include market sector funds, and possibly even leveraged funds. It's likely that the reader will not find the 80 funds currently sponsored by Fidelity. However, the basic four to six funds now in place will be expanded by some insurers to more than a dozen.

However, since liquidity of assets is not as important in these variable products because of the tax ramifications noted in Chapters 7 through 10, the life insurers also are likely to offer illiquid options such as income-producing real estate, and possibly producing oil & gas properties as options.

It is not beyond the realm of possibility that even precious metals or undeveloped land options could fit well in the variable scheme, even though the basic merit and meaning of "insurance," which portrays a picture of powerful guarantees, suffers in the process. After all, life insurers know quite a lot about real estate investment. It seems that the Metropolitan, Prudential, and Equitable life companies own most of the big buildings that dot Main Streets in America. The large life insurers have also dabbled in oil & gas.

Innovation in the variable product area will come fast and furious because there are few policy issuers attempting to capture huge investor assets and market share before Uncle Sam once again rings the gong of large scale-tax reform. Tax changes to reduce or eliminate the special benefits available from these new tax-deferred mutual fund families is likely to come as soon as 1989–90, according to well-placed industry observers and tax specialists.

Thus it will be a free-for-all to get policies written and in place before the deadline. To accomplish that, life insurers with approved policies will be more innovative and quick to move than is characteristic of this breed.

An actuary with a major insurer once noted that "it takes about six years, statistically, to get any changes made in this company, including the size and color of the paper clips we use!" The life insurers with variable policies in place realize that they do not have six years. So, six-week decisions are the order of the day.

We are not in a position to know whether a coming tax change will destroy or merely slightly alter the taxability of assets held in the variable contracts. History reveals that tax-law changes in the life insurance area tend to "grandfather" existing contracts. The tax scenario is changed only for new purchasers. There is no assurance that this grandfathering will occur for the variable life insurance contracts, however.

The tax revenue losses experienced by both federal and state collectors are going to be, simply put, massive. This will be particularly true if we are correct in the assumption that at least $100 billion in assets will shift from taxable mutual fund accounts to variable life policies in the coming 30 months or so.

FIGURE 11–3
Individual Products

Annualized Premium Market Share by Product
62 Companies—Year to Date

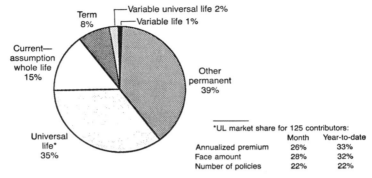

Term 8%
Variable universal life 2%
Variable life 1%
Current—assumption whole life 15%
Other permanent 39%
Universal life* 35%

*UL market share for 125 contributors:

	Month	Year-to-date
Annualized premium	26%	33%
Face amount	28%	32%
Number of policies	22%	22%

Policy Characteristics by Product

		Premium per $1,000	Average size policy	Premium per policy
Term	Month	$ 2.58	$164,586	$ 425
(59 cos.)	Year to date	$ 2.52	$143,503	$ 362
	Year-to-date ratio	94%	109%	103%
Universal life	Month	$11.60	$ 89,874	$1,042
(103 cos.)	Year to date	$11.13	$ 84,581	$ 942
	Year-to-date ratio	99%	100%	99%
Variable life	Month	$22.14	$ 69,916	$1,688
(16 cos.)	Year to date	$22.42	$ 58,950	$1,322
	Year-to-date ratio	121%	114%	139%
Variable	Month	$16.22	$ 99,075	$1,607
universal life	Year to date	$13.65	$ 83,133	$1,135
(14 cos.)	Year-to-date ratio	112%	115%	129%
Current-assumption	Month	$13.91	$ 68,065	$2,172
whole life	Year to date	$19.61	$ 55,595	$1,090
(34 cos.)	Year-to-date ratio	128%	98%	126%
Total sales	Month	$12.38	$ 71,163	$ 881
(125 cos.)	Year to date	$10.59	$ 59,679	$ 632
	Year-to-date ratio	99%	106%	104%

Sales Comparisons with Last Year
Year to Date

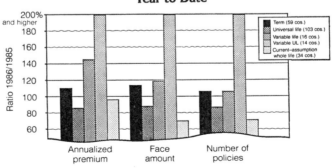

Ratio 1986/1985

Term (59 cos.)
Universal life (103 cos.)
Variable life (16 cos.)
Variable UL (14 cos.)
Current–assumption whole life (34 cos.)

Annualized premium · Face amount · Number of policies

Reprinted with permission from the copyrighted publication "Monthly Survey of Life Insurance Sales in the United States," December 1986.
Source: Life insurance Management & Research Association.

That huge sum, using averages of course, translates into a Federal tax revenue loss on the order of $4 billion yearly, and growing!

That $4 billion loss relates only to assets shifting to variable life from taxable mutual funds. It does not deal with the very real question of new savers and investors attracted to these remarkable new policies. Scane Bowler, chairman of Pioneer Western Corporation, and a sage industry observer, believes that the recent tax law, which reduced or destroyed the IRA savings tool for millions of families and single folks, "could by itself move $100+ billion to (our) variable products!"

But variable life insurance products are not the only innovation in the mutual fund area linked to life insurance. Two of the early combination products involve the issuance of life insurance in conjunction with a simultaneous and systematic purchase of mutual funds. While we discussed these earlier, a quick review is in order.

- The "balanced program" typically uses ordinary or whole life as the conservative medium, and a growth mutual fund as its companion investment. A fixed monthly payment, often drafted directly from the investor's bank account, is split, usually 50-50, to the two financial media. Pioneer Western was an innovator of this approach, which is focused on the systematic savings or long-term accumulation market. Others such as the Keystone Funds and Ozark Life have been active.
- Equity funding uses a fully registered securities product, as does variable life. But the initial investment purchases mutual funds, and loans are created to pay subsequent life insurance premiums as the asset value of the funds (presumably) increases.

However, neither of these has the built-in tax benefits associated with the variable insurance products that "wrap" the modern mutual fund family inside the policy, endowing those assets (presently, at least) with shelter from taxation on dividends, interest earned, capital gains, and transfers from one fund option to another.

But the "yuppie" marketplace is growing like Topsy, and the yuppies are bent on single-decision answers that simplify life.

These folks want to solve multiple problems simultaneously, and also have some real hope of accumulating substantial wealth. The balanced plan is a realistic answer in dealing with these needs. Thus many more life insurance companies are likely to offer programs of this type as a substitute for the very expensive and time-intensive effort of entering the variable life insurance area.

In sharp contrast, the return of the more complex and leveraged equity funding approach represents a different set of circumstances. Equity funding died when the corporation bearing that name ignominiously entered the history books as a fraud in bankruptcy.

The equity funding product, lacking the ability to fully deduct on tax form 1040 the interest charges generated by the loans, is far less attractive on a "total return" basis than was once the case. However, the gamble of risking life insurance protections and guarantees against the leveraged price volatility of the securities markets, is a very real question when we look at how far this bull market in common stocks has come. As we have noted elsewhere, the prospects for massive price corrections—a bear market for stocks and growth mutual funds—will turn to reality at some future point.

Equity-funding-type programs proved to be a disaster in the bear markets of the early and mid-1970s. Yet some life insurers, such as Chubb, Integon, and Pacific Standard Life, seem bent on reviving this type of combination program as the bull market proceeds to capture hordes of new investors.

There are likely to be many varied types of products linking life insurance with mutual funds, and bank-insurance-fund products being arranged in the canyons of Wall Street and insurance company marble towers. The key problem facing readers reviewing these offerings relates to cost versus benefits. A cost is not always to be eschewed as being bad. But a benefit must always be as described: something obviously useful or helpful to the buyer.

By packaging or linking a variety of financial products to accomplish multiple objectives—as is clearly the case with variable life insurance—it is also possible to obscure real risks, or to hide the actual costs associated with purchase and maintenance of the program.

With the computer printout—the key sales and marketing tool for those offering these complex rigs—it is often difficult to determine the actual cost or benefit structure. But, for these linked products, packaging and repackaging will be the name of the game for the balance of this powerful bull market . . . or, at least, until disaster strikes again and all parties return to the table of reality.

LEVERAGE, LEVERAGE, LEVERAGE

Tracing the history of the mutual fund industry, we find that the ideas and concepts used in the life insurance area have crossed over to mutual funds before. Two basic methods of using mutual funds—orderly accumulation of shares in a dollar-cost-averaging program, and buy-and-hold for growth and compounding of lump-sum purchases—were complemented in the late 1950s and early 1960s with an annuity-like program called the withdrawal plan, or "check-a-month" program.

A far more correct description for these programs would have been "equity-risk-annuity." The idea was simple, and supported by two decades of rising stock and mutual fund prices: Why pay a life insurance company a premium for guarantees when stock prices spiral endlessly higher each year? But most of the interest in these plans vanished in the crevasses of the terrible 1973–74 bear market.

That bear market was harsh witness to billions of dollars of retirement-oriented funds being wiped away forever. The level monthly payment to holders of these equity annuities, after all, was being delivered from an ever-shrinking asset base. Each month, in a declining stock market, more mutual fund shares were liquidated to pay the level monthly amount, until no assets remained!

A great mutual fund innovator of the past, King Merrit, was once asked by a elderly lady considering one of these withdrawal plans, "What happens to my monthly check, Mr. Merrit, if the stock market goes way down?" "The King" is said to have responded, "With your final check we also send you a gun!"

Despite the fact that many folks did get their final checks in the crash of 1974, the mutual fund industry is bringing the "check-a-month" idea back. After all, we have indeed experienced a tremendous bull market in stocks. Thus the computer illustrations clearly indicate that these equity annuities are "much better" arrangements than those guaranteed insurance annuity contracts.

Buyer beware! Life insurance companies and Uncle Sam can make guarantees. The only guarantee that the securities markets and mutual funds can make is that they will fluctuate in value. Investors in these instruments can make significant total returns when the market is going in the right direction, up. Conversely, investors can turn a large sum into a much smaller one when the reverse occurs.

But the "smile and dial" stock brokers, financial planners, and related financial hucksters will—as they do today with "riskless" option trading programs, "creditworthy" junk bonds, and a variety of similarly unworthy approaches—be calling retirement communities and zip codes heavily populated with the age-fifty-five-plus group. To these needy folks they tout the virtues of check-a-month mutual fund annuities!

What goes around comes around. In many cases what is new today is merely a reflection of a rehashed or modestly repolished product or concept from yesteryear. The public, brokers and financial planners included, have short memories. However, they were not the financial losers; those folks, poor devils, are either in the cemetery or simply ready to be plucked again.

A few pages earlier we made reference to the recent introduction of short selling programs and margin accounts using mutual funds. The reader should be well reminded that these devices are the ultimate in leverage.

SERVICES, SERVICES, SERVICES

As those who manufacture financial products and services—banks, insurance companies, stock and bond asset managers, thrift depositories, brokerage firms, and the like—move closer together, so do the services and packages of services that they offer.

The money market mutual fund stands as the key evolutionary product created by the mutual fund and brokerage communities for the present era. The money fund, combined with the growing and more flexible mutual fund family and advanced computer techniques, is spawning a generation of "total management" tools for savers and investors. They are "company stores" of finance, if you will. "Send your pay check, indeed all checks received, and we'll do everything. This may include:

- Paying bills as due.
- Keeping all pertinent records.
- Owning and holding mutual funds, and discount trading of stocks and bonds.
- Controlling estate assets, including equity access loans on the family abode or country vacation villa.
- Keeping track of the holder's life, health, and casualty insurance coverages, updating these as required, and paying premiums as due.

Can the Mastercard or Visa, and the easy-access bank teller card, be far behind?

Thus it is possible to picture the home computer linked to the television set and tied via telephone modem into the data bank at one of these futuristic asset management and insurance goliaths. All financial transactions from savings and checking to myriad forms of asset management and trading in individual securities will flow through the system. Retirement plans, trust and estate plans, will be included in the comprehensive package, as will receipt of income from all sources, and comprehensive bill paying. The cashless society will have arrived.

As this new era takes hold, the singular question is clearly cost- and benefit-related. What will the complete set of services cost? How will the saver, investor, or insured determine which service supplier can deliver the largest set of benefits—low-cost banking, competitive asset management for mutual funds or stocks and bonds, and insurance premiums for health, life, and casualty coverages? And will their prices be in the ballpark? It appears to the authors that costs are rising much faster than benefits which, of course, negatively affects the sought-after but often elusive "alpha-plus" total return.

If we look at the world of mutual funds today to evaluate cost of ownership, we get some scary and confusing signals about tomorrow's costs. At one time, for example, there were just load mutual funds, charging a high of 8.5 percent to a low of 1 percent at point of purchase; and there were no-load funds. The selection procedure was simple: either pay a sales charge and get some advice from a presumed professional, or pay no sales charges and make the selection of a fund or fund family from available literature, an advisory service, or a financial magazine reporting quarterly performance figures.

COSTS, COSTS, COSTS

The 1980s have witnessed not only the introduction of one thousand or so new mutual funds, but also virtual elimination of that simple load versus no-load pricing scheme. Today there are so many different configurations in pricing that it takes a financial wizard to unravel the cost of mutual fund ownership.

The culprits are found in the 1980 decision by the Securities and Exchange Commission to allow the 12b-1 plan pricing discussed in Chapters 1 and 2, coupled with a growing trend to increase overall management fees. To exacerbate the weight of these forces, there has been significant growth in what is known as rear-end loading, and funds that are sometimes no-load, and at other times modestly loaded.

Another trend of the moment is the "half-load" idea. If the public doesn't like the 8 percent sales charge, then let's drop from that higher level to 4 percent or so, to see if a lower sales charge reduces buyer reluctance. And so the story goes. Thus what you see isn't always what you get. To complicate the cost issue, the various charges for sales costs and management burdens are not always easily found in the mutual fund prospectus. Worse, some funds in a given family may be loaded in one shape, and others in the same fund family priced quite differently.

Lastly in the area of pricing trends we see the beginnings of "mixed" loading. The mutual fund family offers shares with:

- A small initial sales charge, say 2 percent, or roughly the same amount charged to buy and sell common stocks through a broker.
- The fund also assesses a small rear-end or back load; 1 or 2 percent would be typical.
- The same fund also structures the annual fee as a 12b-1; possibly the expense ratio now swims north of 2 percent.

To the old adage, "they get you comin' and goin'," we now add, "and while you're in residence!" But the trend is there, and these mixed loadings will likely cost the fund shareholder quite a bit more over the long term than was paid under the old scheme. After all, the great bull market in stocks has produced incredible returns for many mutual funds. Equipped with pretty sales literature describing the riches won for fund investors, the management companies that sponsor the funds are looking for ways to levy heftier charges at all points in the sales and management process.

REGULATION AND TAXES

The Securities & Exchange Commission is studying this total confusion in mutual fund pricing. *The New York Times,* in a recent feature in the Sunday "Personal Finance" column, headlined the problem as "Those Tricky Mutual Fund Costs!" Uncle Sam is aware of the problem, as are many of the major financial publications.

The mutual fund investor may possibly expect redress through standardized cost and benefit illustrations in the offering prospectus, and bundling of all costs in one place in that all-important document. If not, the professional arbitrators and courtrooms soon will be overloaded with litigation involving lack of full disclosure. As we suggested in Chapter 1, ask for and get, with the fund salesperson's signature, a summary disclosure of all costs—everything that you will pay in loads (both in and out), 12b-1, and management fees.

The tax picture vis-à-vis mutual funds at large, and more specifically variable life insurance products, will likely also change. The changes will come rather swiftly if we are correct in our assumption that hundreds of billions of dollars will shift from taxable funds to these wonderful tax-deferral vehicles in the next two years.

The revenue loss to Uncle Sam and state tax collectors, as noted earlier, will be huge. We see nothing in the 1986 tax act's projections for tax-income loss that focuses even remotely on this very large hole in the law. Obviously, all taxpayers who do not own one of these variable shelters are going to pay the freight for those who do. And, unlike the tax shelters dealt a death blow in the latest tax bill, these variable products fit the protection needs and risk tolerance for many millions of taxpayers, not just the few that ventured into movie deals, equipment leasing, cattle breeding, and leveraged shopping centers.

Our best guess is that Congress will need the 1988 session to determine the extent of revenue losses, and a year or so of haggling and lobbying before the guns of change are loaded and fired.

CONCLUSIONS

The market of stocks can go higher from present levels and interest rates can continue to decline. In that heady atmosphere the booming mutual fund and variable insurance areas will continue to innovate new products apace. These new ideas will be speculative as investors attempt to reach for the moon, and product sponsors accommodate those investors searching for heady profits.

These riskier investment vehicles, coupled with the boom in sector funds, will lead to the next great stock market tumble. In that downer, the balance sheets for many of the latecomers will see a real haircut, and tax losses will abound. A shake-out will occur in the mutual fund industry as a result. In that shake-out only the strong will survive.

Broadening of mutual fund and variable product offerings will extend to services as well as pure products. Will the fund family and insurance sponsors offer free computers and modems for larger full-service accounts? Such is already the case in the discount brokerage area, so why not the huge life insurers and major mutual fund families?

But the important game at hand is in the pricing area. Already the boggle of present approaches—no-load, load, low-load, 12b-1, mixed, back-end, etc.—is being tested in many variations. The variations will be designed to keep the fund shareholder off-balance and leave more of the holder's money on the sponsor's table.

Regulatory change, while overdue, will be slow in coming. The Boesky/insider-trading mess on Wall Street, coupled with the flood of paperwork associated with issuance of new securities in this bull market, and federal spending constraints, have put a lot of pressure on the thinly staffed regulatory bodies.

Taxes will rise. Also the tax pet in this book—variable life insurance—will see more tax exposure. A general tax increase, and loss of generous tax preference for the life insurance industry at large, are two bets on which the authors feel they cannot lose!

Billy Rose admonished us to not invest if the investment eats or needs repairs. The incredible growth in complexity in the mutual fund industry can only lead to a time of painful repair . . . for shareholders as well as the mutual fund sponsors.

INDEX